APOSTOLIC Signs and Gifts OF THE SPIRIT

The Cessation of Miracle Workers During the First Century

GARY W. DERICKSON

LAMPION
House Publishing

LAMPION HOUSE PUBLISHING, LLC
Navasota, Texas 77868
2023

Apostolic Signs and Gifts of the Spirit:
The Cessation of Miracle Workers During the First Century

Copyright © 2023 Gary W. Derickson

All rights reserved.

No part of this book may be reproduced in any form or by any electronic or mechanical means including information storage and retrieval systems, without permission in writing from the author. The only exception is by a reviewer, who may quote short excerpts in a review.

Lampion House Publishing, LLC
P.O. Box 1295
Navasota, TX 77868
Website: http://lampionhousepublishing.com/

ISBN: 979-8-9878598-7-2 (softcover)

Cover and Interior Design/Formatting by Vickie Swisher, Studio 20|20

Printed in the United States of America

To my parents, Glen Sr. and Christiana Derickson, whose faith in Christ and faithfulness to Him motivated me from my childhood till today.

CONTENTS

Foreword.. ix

1: Introduction.. 1

2: The Debate About Modern Faith Healing................... 23

3: Theological Arguments
   For The Cessation Of Miraculous Gifts................... 57

4: Biblical Arguments
   For The Cessation Of Miraculous Gifts................... 75

5: Historical Arguments
   For The Cessation Of Miraculous Gifts................... 101

6: Paul's Inability To Heal................................ 123

7: The Occurrence And Significance Of Miracles Today....... 139

8: Conclusion... 145

Bibliography... 151

Appendix 1: Problems of the Study........................ 165

Appendix 2: Significance of the Study.................... 167

Appendix 3: The Procedure of the Study................... 169

FOREWORD

I appreciate the opportunity to write a foreword for Dr. Gary Derickson's book *Apostolic Signs and Gifts of the Spirit*, which provides a helpful and needed balance that is often lacking in some circles of the Christian community. When one reads the New Testament, it is evident that God worked many miracles through the apostles, and within the New Testament church, various gifts of the Spirit were performed of a miraculous nature. Due to the evidence of these miraculous events, it is assumed by many Christians today that all of these are to be performed and practiced in the contemporary church. Dr. Derickson follows a balanced approach to this controversy, demonstrating that the ability of the apostles to do miracles in the New Testament period gradually subsided by the end of the first century, though not denying that God worked miracles throughout the history of the church according to His own purposes in the lives of His people.

I have observed through the years various Christian leaders who claimed a variety of miracles, and yet were not consistent in their own lives. As well I have been involved in Christian churches and groups who advocated numerous miracles among the people of God, looking down on those who did not. The measured and balanced approach of Gary Derickson is a refreshing study of the biblical text. I have no hesitation in encouraging anyone concerned and uninformed about the thesis of this book to read it to ensure for themselves an appreciation for the purposes of God in doing miracles in His world and among Christians that glorify Him and express care for His people.

H. Wayne House, Th.D., J.D.
Distinguished Research Professor of Theology, Law, and Culture
Faith International University, and Seminary

1

Introduction

At the birth of the church the apostles and others among the first generation of Christians could be viewed as miracle workers. They had authority from God to heal at will and exercised that authority. There are several persons today who profess to exercise the same kind of authority and claim some measure of authority or ability to miraculously heal people similar to the apostles. In recent years even within non-charismatic churches, a willingness to accept the possibility of miracle workers today is growing. As biblical illiteracy increases in the churches, the desire to debate the issue seems to decline. The younger, post-modern generation is less willing to take a stand for or against the issue. Instead, they are more willing to allow the possibility because of their valuation of personal experience over absolutes. So how are we to address this issue today? Can we be dogmatic? How should we relate to those who disagree with us or are unwilling to take a stand on the issue? The answer lies in the evidence of church history as well as the information we can learn from the biblical record, not only in Acts but in the epistles as well. Finally, the work of the Spirit in the church today, in non-Charismatic as well as Pentecostal/Charismatic churches does speak to the issue.

APOSTOLIC *Signs and Gifts* OF THE SPIRIT

To this date, the debate continues within the evangelical community concerning the possibility of present-day miracles and miracle workers. The range of opinion is spread between those who believe that God continues to work miracles today in the same manner and numbers as the first century and those who see miracles as a first-century phenomenon. Between those views are those who are open to miraculous gifts but cautious about their use in the church. This range of views was described well in the book, *Are Miraculous Gifts for Today?* from Zondervan's Counterpoints series.[1] So, what questions should we address today?

It is not the intention of this book to address every area of the modern faith-healing debate. Rather, this book is written to provide questions and answers based on the testimony of Scripture, which challenges specific claims of that movement. It is easy to claim that God wants to heal everybody and that healing is in the atonement. But how well can such claims stand in the face of unhealed saints of the Bible, men who walked with Paul, who had healed others earlier in his ministry?

In 1954 a man named Charles Braden published an article based on a survey of several major denominations. In it, he reported that miraculous healings were being attempted in large numbers of non-charismatic churches.[2] His report revealed a general movement of churchmen seeking to grapple with the healing claims and demands faced by their churches. The Spring 1985 issue of *Leadership* magazine devoted itself to the question of the healing ministry of the church and included articles fa-

---

[1] Wayne Grudem, ed. *Are Miraculous Gifts for Today?* Counterpoints, Grand Rapids: Zondervan Publishing House, 1966.

[2] Charles S. Braden, "Study of Spiritual Healing in the Churches," *Pastoral Psychology* 5: 44 (May 1954): 9-15.

voring miraculous healing as a normal experience in the church.[3] More recently, Craig Keener has argued for the continuance of miraculous healings throughout history and to this day.[4]

In the 1960s and 70s, with the spread of the Pentecostal movement into the broad evangelical community, various spokesmen for the movement promoted the idea of miracles being the normal experience of the church. Further, some claimed to be miracle workers. For example, Kenneth Copeland taught that miracles should be experienced today throughout the church. He also held to the existence of modern prophets and apostles.[5] Oral Roberts was perhaps the most famous advocate of this position. In his 1975 book entitled *A Daily Guide to Miracles*, he said: "Jesus indicates a miracle is not a sometime or onetime thing. … Now the moment you stop calling them miracles and put them into the area of the works of God, then you see that Jesus Christ has only come to do what God has been doing all through the centuries and will do forever."[6]

In the 80s and 90s, new figures arose in the miracle, or as it is now being called, the Signs and Wonders movement. The most prominent was John Wimber, pastor of the Vineyard Church in Anaheim, California. The Vineyard movement presents signs and wonders as a normal experience of the church.[7] Wimber authored two books espousing his views, entitled *Power Evangelism* and *Power Healing*. Kraft, a Wimber associate at Fuller's

---

[3] *Leadership* 6: 2 (Spring 1985). The July 11, 1986, issue of *Christianity Today*, when reporting on worldwide church growth, began its article by recounting a "miraculous" healing in China which led to the salvation of the person healed. Miracles were identified as a key to the Pentecostal success in evangelizing the largely animistic cultures of the third world, especially Latin America (Sharon E. Mumper, "Where in the World Is the Church Growing?" *Christianity Today* 30: 10 [July 11, 1986]: 17, 21).

[4] Craig S. Keener, *Miracles: The Credibility of the New Testament Accounts*, Vols. 1 & 2 (Grand Rapids: Baker, 2011).

[5] Kenneth Copeland, *Walking in the Realm of the Miraculous* (Fort Worth: KCP Publications, 1979), 64-65.

[6] Oral Roberts, *A Daily Guide to Miracles* (Old Tappan: Fleming H. Revell Company, 1975), 190-91.

[7] Tim Stafford, "Testing the Wine from John Wimber's Vineyard," *Christianity Today*, 30: 11 (August 8, 1986): 17, 18, 20.

School of World Missions, wrote, "I don't believe that miracles ever have been absent from our culture. I think our eyes have been clouded over so that we haven't seen things. When people open themselves up to more of the miraculous, I feel that God gives it to them."[8] Another significant figure was C. Peter Wagner who, while refusing to be identified as either a "Pentecostal" or a "Charismatic,"[9] supported the Vineyard Movement and wrote: "The power that worked in Jesus for His miraculous ministry not only is related to the power available to us today; it is exactly the same. As we relate to God in prayer, faith and obedience we have abundant resources to go forth in Jesus' name to preach everywhere 'with signs following' as did the early disciples."[10] Samuel Storms, defending a Pentecostal view of miraculous gifts referred to those who did not lay hands on people for their healing as "functional deists."[11]

This idea that signs and wonders should accompany the preaching of the gospel even today is echoed by others.[12] Paul Beals has observed that this emphasis has resulted in certain men going to "excesses in an effort to prove that they, at least, have the apostolic power."[13] Further, groups such as the Bay Area Skeptics and the Committee for the Scientific Examination of Religion have investigated men such as Peter Popoff, David Paul, and W. V. Grant and documented evidence that they actively engage in deception rather than truth when they promote themselves as

---

[8] Wimber is quoted in an article compiled by Karen Ball, "An Evaluation by Theologians," Christian Life 44: 6 (October 1982): 67.

[9] C. Peter Wagner, "Healing Without Hassle," Leadership 6: 2 (Spring 1985): 114-15.

[10] Wagner, "The Power of God and Your Power," Christian Life 45: 3 (July 1983): 46.

[11] C. Samuel Storms, "Third Wave View" in Are Miraculous Gifts for Today? Counterpoints (Grand Rapids: Zondervan Publishing House, 1996), 214.

[12] William F. Bryan, "Miraculous Continuity," The Alliance Witness 114: 2 (January 24, 1979): 3-4; Charles E. Carlston, "The Question of Miracles," Andover Newton Quarterly 12: 2 (November 1971): 99-107; J. Rodman Williams, The Gift of the Holy Spirit Today (Plainfield: Logos International, 1980), 59.

[13] Paul A. Beals, "The Significance of Miracles" (ThM thesis, DTS, 1952), 58.

healers.[14]

The modern faith healing movement's arguments are generally based either on the concept of healing being in the atoning death of Christ[15] or that God must work in the same way today as He did in the first-century church.[16]

In contrast to the modern miracle movement are those who see miracles declining in the first century as the church became established, the Scriptures were completed, and the apostolic miracle workers either died or were martyred.[17] John F. Walvoord, the Chancellor of Dallas Theological Seminary, expressing this view, said, "After the ascension of Christ into heaven, miraculous works continued in the early church, on many occasions attendant the preaching of the Word and constituting proof that it was indeed from God. With the completion of the

---

14 See the Summer 1986 issue of *Free Inquiry* magazine (Vol. 6, No. 3) for articles on these men. Peter Popoff's deceptions are especially well documented. In the cases of these men, it could be argued from the evidence provided that their public declarations in no way match up with their inner convictions. Though they preach about miracles, in actuality they are nothing more than con artists, wolves in sheep's clothing.

15 Dennis Bennet, "Does God Want to Heal Everybody?" *Charisma* 9: 2 (September 1983): 59; Peder Borgen, "Miracles of Healing in the New Testament," *Studia Theologica* 35 (1981): 101; Pat Robertson, *My Prayer for You* (Old Tappan: Fleming H. Revell Company, 1977), 57, 64; Ken Sumrall, "Miracles and Healing," in *The Holy Spirit in Today's Church*, ed. Erling Jorstad (Nashville: Abingdon Press, 1973), 105-108.

16 Herald Bresden with James F. Scheer, *Need a Miracle?* (Old Tappan: Fleming H. Revell Company, 1979), 16; Nick Cavnar, "Miracles: Do They Really Happen?" *New Covenant* 12: 4 (November 1982): 5; Robert C. Dalton, *Tongues Like as of Fire* (Springfield: The Gospel Publishing House, 1945), 119; A. De Groot, *The Bible on Miracles* (Trans. Jos A. Roessen. De Pere: St. Norbert Abbey Press, 1966), 13; Christiaan De Wet, "Biblical Basis of Signs and Wonders," *Christian Life* 44: 6 (October 1982): 28; Guy Duffield and Nathaniel M. Van Cleave, *Foundations of Pentecostal Theology* (Los Angeles: L. I. F. E. Bible College, 1983), 377-84, 388-92; Douglas A. Oss, "A Pentecostal/Charismatic View," in *Are Miraculous Gifts for Today? Four Views*, Counterpoints (Grand Rapids: Zondervan Publishing House, 1996), 275; G. Aiken Taylor, "Miracles—Yes or No?" *The Presbyterian Journal* 33: 16 (August 14, 1974): 7-9; Ernest Gordon recounts in his book, *The Fact of Miracle* (Francestown: Marshall Jones Company, 1955), "documented" occurrences which are supernatural and parallel to biblical miracles. Through this he then argues for the present continuance of miracles from God.

17 Robert Anderson, *The Silence of God* (New York: Dodd Mead & Company, 1897), 18; Thomas R. Edgar, *Miraculous Gifts: Are They for Today?* (Neptune: Loizeaux Brothers, 1983), 260; Henry W. Frost, *Miraculous Healing* (New York: Fleming H. Revell Company, 193139), 127-29; A. C. Gaebelein, *The Acts of the Apostles* (New York: Publication Office "Our Hope," n.d.), 146; John B. Graber, "The Temporary Gifts of the Holy Spirit" (ThM thesis, DTS, 1947), 56; C. Everett Koop, "Faith Healing and the Sovereignty of God," *Tenth: An Evangelical Quarterly* (July 1976): 62; Rolland D. McCune, "A Biblical Study of Tongues and Miracles," *Central Bible Quarterly* 19: 3 (Fall 1976): 19; John Phillips, "Miracles: Not for Today," *Moody Monthly* 82: 11 (July-August 1982): 73.

New Testament, the need for such miraculous evidence in support of the preached Word seems to have ceased, and the authority and convincing power of the Spirit seems to have replaced these outer manifestations."[18]

Those who see miracles declining in the first century generally base their views on one or more of three ideas. First, they understand Hebrews 2 to be teaching that miracles had already passed off of the scene.[19] Second, some point to the fact that the latter epistles are basically silent concerning miracles.[20] Finally, some have argued that Paul's inability to heal three friends indicates a loss of miraculous power.[21] Though he understands the command of Jesus in Luke 10:17-20 to mean that all missionaries should be able to perform miracles, Fridrichsen continues to argue for the disappearance of miracles between the writing of 1 Corinthians and the pastoral epistles.[22]

Both sides of the debate would claim to be biblical, though one must be mistaken. This book is an attempt to help clarify the issue further by examining the position that miracles did not just decline in the first century. Instead, the evidence provided here is sufficient to argue forcibly that within the record of the New Testament, there is evidence of an end to miracle workers, beginning with Paul.

The Confusion about Miracles

A part of the difficulty within today's debate lies in the vast differences in each position's definition of a miracle. Often the two

---

18 John F. Walvoord, *The Holy Spirit at Work Today* (Chicago: Moody Press, 1973), 43-44.
19 Charles C. Ryrie, "Greater Works Than These," *Good News Broadcaster* 41: 6 (June 1983): 33; Paul E. Sywulka, "The Contribution of Hebrews 2:3-4 to the Problem of Apostolic Miracles" (ThM thesis, DTS, 1967) 47.
20 John L. Booth, "The Purpose of Miracles" (ThM thesis, DTS, 1982) 202-203.
21 Ada R. Habershon, *The Study of the Miracles* (London: Pickering & Inglis, n.d.), 240, 242; Ryrie, "Greater Works Than These," 34.
22 Anton Fridrichsen, *The Problem of Miracle in Primitive Christianity* (Trans. by Roy A. Harrisville and John S. Hanson. Minneapolis: Augsburg Publishing House, 1972), 135, 147.

groups are talking "apples and oranges" and so are fighting different issues. For example, some conservative Evangelicals who do not hold to miracle workers are accused of being anti-supernatural or denying all miracles. Yet, this is only rarely the case. Few, if any, Evangelicals doubt that God either can or does intervene today in miraculous ways. The issue for them is more whether He does it through men or simply answers prayer, sometimes with a miracle. This makes it necessary to propose a definition that clarifies what miracles are being examined in the books of the New Testament. Benjamin B. Warfield, in arguing against modern miracles, identified them with the apostles and their generation. He linked miracles to the gifts of the Spirit and saw their purpose as authenticating the validity of the apostles and the witnesses of their generation. From this assumption, he then argued against modern miracle workers based on the gospel and its bearers no longer needing to prove they are from God. Also, he argued that history has indicated that miracles ceased with the first-century generation of Christians.[23]

In contrast to his position, we have men such as C. Peter Wagner and Oral Roberts claiming that miracles and miracle workers have continued and can be presently experienced within the modern Church. But, in contrast to Warfield's linking miracles to spiritual gifts and authentication of God's first messengers, Oral Roberts defines them as entirely different: "A miracle to one person might not be a miracle to another. To most of us, a miracle is something happening that we can't explain, but that makes a profound change for the better in our lives. I have known many miracles, both of a completely extraordinary nature and of a nature that I alone might appreciate."[24] Thus, for Oral Roberts, the individual is free to determine if he or she considers something miraculous. This is convenient since one can claim to

---

23 Benjamin B. Warfield, *Counterfeit Miracles* (New York: Charles Scribner's Sons, 1918), 5-6.
24 Roberts, *Daily Guide*, 139.

have experienced a miracle if he only reduces the miraculous to anything unusual or beneficial to his desires. This definition is weak since it cheapens a miracle. A miracle is a supernatural act of God, whether directly or through the agency of a person, that affects the material world. A miracle worker is someone given authority by God to intervene supernaturally, such as the apostles and Philip the Evangelist (Acts 8:4-8).

It is illegitimate to accuse non-charismatic Evangelicals of denying miracles. Men such as Henry W. Frost, while arguing against modern miracle-working, recognize that God still does perform miraculous healings in answer to prayer, though not always. For example, Frost himself says, "It is not, therefore, the age of miracles, except as God is pleased to manifest His power to individuals, in exceptional circumstances, and for specific purposes."[25] Charles C. Ryrie agrees with him and sees God still performing miracles today. Even so, he holds to the miraculous gifts being passed since their purpose of authenticating God's message and messengers is no longer needed.[26] It is clear that one's definition of a miracle necessarily leads him or her to one of several positions concerning miracles. So, in order that readers from every position on this issue may clearly understand the arguments of this book, a clear and precise definition of what a miracle is must be given.

This is where the "rubber meets the road" in much of the debate on miracles. If everyone were talking about the same thing, it would be easier to know whom to ignore and whom to heed. So that there is no confusion concerning what constitutes a miracle, an extensive working definition needs to be developed. This should clarify that a difference exists between supernatural interventions by God in answer to prayer and "miracles" that certain men are claiming to perform. In this discussion there is no in-

---

25   Frost, *Miraculous Healing*, 6, 117.
26   Ryrie, *The Holy Spirit* (Chicago: Moody Press, 1965), 87.

tention to use the word miracle negatively or disparage miracle workers. Paul was a miracle worker, as was Peter and the other apostles. God worked miracles through other miracle workers in the first-century Church. Organic diseases were healed. Dead people—not unconscious or comatose, but medically dead—had their lives restored to them. Dorcas had really died before Peter resurrected her (Acts 9:36-43), and Eutychus was completely dead after falling from the window and before being raised by Paul (Acts 20:7-12).

What is a Miracle?

So, what is a miracle? Keener addresses this question and suggests that "miracle" can be a broader category than just something impossible happening. He sees divine interventions through natural phenomena as miracles because of their divine initiation and timing. This is God "working through the created order." He rejects the idea that miracles be defined solely in terms of the "violation of nature."[27] Booth defines a miracle more narrowly: "In the Bible a miracle is an observable phenomenon effected directly or indirectly by supernatural power in which the laws of nature are not suspended or violated, but a supernatural power outside of nature intervenes with new effect for a specific purpose."[28] This definition is adequate for miracles when used for all supernatural events. Yet, it is too broad when considering signs performed by men such as the apostles. Sywulka defined apostolic miracles as "the miracles in the early church, which were wrought primarily by the apostles in order to confirm them and their message, and which were directly effective at the agents' will."[29] Thus he added the element of the agent's choice of time and place, making him an active participant in the event and not simply a passive chan-

---

27 Keener, *Miracles*, 181.
28 Booth, "The Purpose of Miracles," 8.
29 Sywulka, "Contribution of Hebrews 2:3-4," 14.

nel through which God worked. Norman Geisler describes miracles as "out-of-the-ordinary" events that have theological, moral, doctrinal, and teleological dimensions. They "stand in contrast to nature" and have a "supernatural cause."[30] He defines miracles as "always successful," with "immediate" results and "no relapses," that "confirm God's spokesman."[31] Wayne Grudem, on the other hand, objects to his definition as "too restrictive" and defines miracles as "a less common kind of God's activity in which he arouses people's awe and wonder and bears witness to himself."[32]

For this book, the miracles under consideration involve an agent through whom they are worked. A more technical definition would be that "Miracles are supernatural acts of God that He sometimes chooses to perform through the agency of someone gifted with miraculous authority." Only those supernatural acts worked through an agent, such as the apostles and apostolic generation, or men today with similar authority (and ability to demonstrate that authority and power at will), are considered miracles by miracle workers. This definition is selected since the issue of modern miracles ultimately focuses on the question of the present-day occurrence of miracle workers rather than the question of God's ability. This definition does not imply that God no longer intervenes supernaturally and answers prayer on behalf of His own. Sywulka expresses the point in question well when he says, "It should be noted that the issue is not whether God works miracles today, for all Evangelicals agree that He does. It is rather whether He works them through individuals today in the same way as He did in Acts."[33] Though they are miracles by definition, revelation, and visions such as the Apostle John experienced are not included in this study. In this regard, Chantry's

---

30 Norman L. Geisler, "Miracle," *Baker Encyclopedia of Christian Apologetics*, Baker Reference Library (Grand Rapids: Baker Books, 1999), 451.
31 Norman Geisler, *Signs and Wonders* (Wheaton: Tyndale House, 1988), 28-30.
32 Wayne Grudem, *Systematic Theology*, 2nd ed. (Grand Rapids: Zondervan Academic, 2020), 470, 482.
33 Ibid., 15.

definition is preferred in which he says: "In a precise definition of the term, we must refer only to works of God which are observable to human senses, uncommon to human experience, and very rare. Usual workings of God in this world may be quite as much the effects of God's power as are miracles, but to be accurate, we must refer to His normal acts as providence rather than miracle."[34] This would then make God's answers to prayer acts of providence rather than miracles, even when supernaturally accomplished. Thus, holding a position that first-century caliber miracles are not occurring, if any, does not necessitate an anti-supernatural understanding of God's working in the world today. It only asks the question, are there men today who possess and express miracle-working authority within themselves? So, this discussion of the issue limits its definition of miracles to those supernatural acts worked through a human agent.

A good working definition of a miracle should include its inability to be repeated through human agency, such as medical practices or the power of the mind over the body. This very aspect of the miraculous is what drove nineteenth-century liberal theologians to reject the miracles of the Bible. In their estimation, miracles were impossible because they were not repeatable. Thus, they could not be confirmed through scientific experimentation and therefore could not happen. However, we should embrace such a definition of the miraculous. The miraculous, by its very nature, should *not* be repeatable. They should involve an effect on the natural world, including the human body, that cannot be achieved by any human means. This does not mean that if an organic disease, such as melanoma cancer, can be cured by radiation and chemotherapy, God cannot miraculously heal that person. Rather, taking such an example, miraculous healing of melanoma must necessarily *not* involve medical intervention and *not* be attributable to the natural phenomenon of remission re-

---

34 Walter G. Chantry, *Signs of the Apostles* (Carlisle: The Banner of Truth Trust, 1973), 13.

sulting from the body suddenly producing antibodies that kill the tumor. This means that it is only a miracle if a person's melanoma disappears instantly and without medical intervention or the body fighting it off through its own resources. If, after prayer, a patient slowly goes into remission, we can recognize this as an answer to prayer. However, that healing will still be the product of natural processes rather than miraculous intervention. This contrast between biological processes and instantaneous divine intervention can be seen in Jesus' healing ministry. The illnesses recounted were organic diseases for which there was no cure in their day, such as leprosy or blindness. The healing occurred instantaneously and visibly, not gradually or subtly. When Jesus healed Peter's mother-in-law, not only did her fever leave her immediately, but she was instantly able to get up and serve her guests (Matt 8:14-15). Her recovery was measurable and visible to all around. It was not psychosomatic.

The "healing" of psychosomatic illnesses is not miraculous. A disease caused by the mind can be cured by the mind. And many "diseases" are the body's response to stress, anxiety, or mental states. Convincing the person they have been "healed" may cause the mind to bring the body back into alignment in that area, make the pain go away, or make the organ function more normally, but without being miraculous. Thus, in discerning whether a miracle has occurred, we must evaluate a range of evidence. However, that being said, when encountering a psychosomatic illness in a person, we should never settle for alleviating the symptom. That person needs to address the emotional or spiritual issue that triggered the physical response in the first place. If not, a new problem is likely to arise in the person's body as the mind attempts to distract itself from the real issue. The human being is a complexity of interactions between the spirit, soul, and body. Though not always, there can be very direct cause-effect relationships between the spirit and body. We see this in the teaching of Scripture. For example, Proverbs teaches us, "Do not be wise in your own eyes; fear the LORD and depart from evil. It will be health to your flesh, and strength to your bones" (Prov 3:7-8), and "A sound heart *is* life to the body, but envy is rottenness to the bones" (Prov 14:30). Further, "A merry heart does good, *like* medicine, but a broken spirit dries the bones" (Prov 17:22). Thus, we can see the relationship of emotions and will to health.

Does rapid healing constitute a miraculous intervention by God? Again, I would say not especially. If we have examples elsewhere of that same disease responding to emotional stimuli, we may conclude God's blessing on the person's natural healing process without calling it a miracle. If a person recovers quickly, let's say over a week rather than taking months, we may conclude it reflects God's blessing and their body's response to a change of heart or forgiveness of sin (Jas 5:15), not a miraculous intervention. If, on the other hand, the person we pray for is instantly cured in a way not possible, even in unusually fast natural healing cases, we should conclude that God chose to give instant relief miraculously. God's miraculous intervention may involve causing something to happen instantly, which usually takes months. The speeding up of the healing process beyond what is possible for the human body would be miraculous. Again, look at Peter's mother-in-law. She could have recovered from her fever in another week or so and eventually regained her strength enough to serve without Jesus' intervention. Jesus' miraculous intervention did more than remove the virus or bacteria causing the fever. It restored her body's tissues and energy supply to a condition as if she had never had the disease instantly. In the same way, when Jesus raised Jairus's daughter, she not only got up from her deathbed but woke up hungry (Mark 5:43)! She was returned to a state of normality characteristic of a healthy young girl.

When evaluating claims of miracles, especially involving healing, the return to normality must be evident, not a movement toward or partial experience of normality. The lame man healed by Peter and John did more than stand up and shuffle along. Instead, he continued to walk with them in the temple and leaped while praising God (Acts 3:8-9). That would require not only his ankles and feet to be strengthened but his leg muscles to be strengthened to the point of functioning normally. Since he had not walked since birth, we would expect that his leg muscles would be mostly atrophied and certainly not toned in any way. To walk *and* repeatedly leap necessarily means that the healing of his feet and ankles included strengthening leg muscles to a state of existence that would have resulted from normal life activities. And, again, it resulted instantly, not from days or months of physical therapy and exercise.

In summary, as we evaluate claims of miracles, we must insist on the impossibility of the event apart from divine intervention. Also, we should not be eager to attribute anything and everything to God's miraculous intervention, no matter how it might help "enhance" our message or "glorify" God. As said earlier, God is only glorified by the truth, not by false claims. We do not do God a service by promoting as true things that are not true of Him. At the same time, we also do not do Him service by denying what is true about Him. If He has intervened miraculously, we have an obligation to both recognize it and praise Him for it.

Is the Exercise of a Spiritual Gift Miraculous?

The question of the relationship of spiritual gifts to miracles needs addressing at this point. Leslie Flynn defines a spiritual gift as "a divinely ordained spiritual ability through which Christ enables His church to execute its task on earth."[35] I would define them as supernatural enablements the Holy Spirit gives, in which the person receiving the gift consciously participates in its exercise. Though the miracle worker is acting in dependence on the Holy Spirit, the action taken involves the will of the miracle

---

35   Leslie B. Flynn, *19 Gifts of the Spirit* (Wheaton, IL: Victor Books, 1994) 26.

worker in choosing to act. The results of the exercise of at least some of the spiritual gifts mentioned in 1 Corinthians should be recognized as miraculous. These would include some of the so-called "sign" gifts as they are described by many today. And, if someone had certain of those gifts, they should and would have been considered a miracle worker. And it should be noted that there were miracle workers in the early church. It was one of the spiritual gifts listed by Paul in 1 Corinthians 12. However, it was not "a given" that anyone with enough faith could work miracles. Thus, we have Paul's rhetorical question, "Are all workers of miracles?" (1 Cor 12:29), with the required answer of "No, not all are workers of miracles."[36]

The non-miraculous spiritual gifts are still supernaturally enabled, being worked in the life of the recipient by the Holy Spirit. A gift such as the word of wisdom (1 Cor 12:8) would enable its recipient to speak beyond themselves as enabled by the Holy Spirit but would not be miraculous. The church body would benefit from the guidance the gifted person could provide, who would thereby be an agent through whom the Holy Spirit blessed others in that body. Similarly, none of the gifts listed in Romans 12:6-8 involve the performance of miracles unless one counts prophesying as miraculous, which one should not. Even so, though not every spiritual gift need be miraculous, there were those gifts that involved miraculous acts.

The Goal of This Book

This book aims to evaluate and discuss the evidence within Scripture that supports the claim of a decline in the number of miracles in the first century. Also, it seeks to determine if Paul's three friends can be used as a part of that argument or whether their healings were not accomplished for some other reason.

---

36 The question uses the negative particle, mē (μὴ πάντες δυνάμεις;) in the question, thus requiring a negative response (William D. Mounce, Basics of Biblical Greek, 3rd ed. [Grand Rapids: Zondervan, 2009], 295).

The Importance of Demonstrating a Decline

Some consider miracles a necessary element in God's present work within the body of Christ. Others see them as a part of the transitional framework of the first-century Church whose usefulness and occurrence passed with the apostles' generation and completion of the canon. Both cannot be correct. So, how can we determine which is the better view? Part of the answer is to determine the possibility or level of probability that miracles declined in the first century. Did they end with either the apostles or the first generation of believers? If so, why? Was their usefulness over? Was their discontinuance a part of God's plan? If so, what in Scripture would tell us that?

A decline or cessation of miracles within the first century has been argued based on several lines of evidence. First, the necessity for their decline has been demonstrated theologically from the purpose of miracles as authenticating God's messengers.[37] "It was the sign-gift of the apostles, but since the apostolate was a temporary function, that which served as its credential likewise passed away as a matter of course."[38] The reference to miracles in Hebrews 2:1-5 has also proven useful to this line of argument.[39] Second, the decline has been argued based on the place of miracles in revelation. Sywulka states this position: "As long as the gospel was transmitted only by word of mouth, miracles were a necessity. The true message needed certification to distinguish it from false messages. Today, however, the one true message has been recorded permanently in the inspired Scriptures. These carry their proof of trustworthiness and need no miraculous attestation."[40] With a belief in the closing of the canon then comes an understanding that miracles must necessarily have ceased with

---

[37] Graham H. Twelftree, *Paul and the Miraculous: A Historical Reconstruction* (Grand Rapids: Baker Academic, 2013) 90.

[38] Graber, "Temporary Gifts," 65.

[39] Beals, "Significance of Miracles," 53; Frost, *Miraculous Healing*, 124-25.

[40] Sywulka, "Contribution of Hebrews 2:3-4," 42.

its completion. Third, evidence within the record of history indicates a lack of miracles within the years immediately following the end of the apostolic age.[41] Miracles then began to reappear in later centuries. Warfield observes: "There is little or no evidence at all for miracle-working during the first fifty years of the post-Apostolic church; it is slight and unimportant for the next fifty years; it grows more abundant during the next century (the third); and it becomes abundant and precise only in the fourth century, to increase still further in the fifth and beyond."[42] This position is opposed by those holding to modern miracle workers, though, with the same church fathers being quoted by both those arguing for an end to miracles and those arguing for their continuance.[43] Lockyer seeks to invalidate any post-apostolic claims of miracles by saying, "There is record of miraculous cures in the Church after the first century, but miracles were not recorded under inspired guidance like the miracles of the apostolic age."[44] Rather than arguing about whether miracles were occurring, the question needs to be framed around miracle workers. God has been miraculously intervening in the lives of His children since the earliest days of mankind. After all, Enoch being taken alive to heaven must be recognized as miraculous (Gen 5:21-24). Lines of evidence, such as the writings of the early church fathers, though useful, are not conclusive. Instead, evidence or argument from the biblical record seems a better source for strengthening the position that miracle workers ceased.

Demonstrating a noticeable decline, if not measurable, within the record of Scripture would significantly strengthen the position of those holding to a cessation of miracles within the

---

41 Erroll Hulse, "Can We Do Miracles Today?" *The Banner of Truth* 214 (July 1981): 26.
42 Warfield, Counterfeit Miracles, 9-10.
43 Ibid, 25-31; A. J. Gordon, The Ministry of Healing (New York: Fleming H. Revell Company, 1882), 237-42; Charles Hummel, "Healing: Our Double Standard?" Christian Life 44: 7 (November 1982): 33; John C. Whitcomb, "Does God Want Christians to Perform Miracles Today?" Grace Journal 12: 3 (Fall 1971): 10-12.
44 Herbert Lockyer, All the Miracles of the Bible (Grand Rapids: Zondervan, 1961), 19.

first century. This would provide empirical evidence in support of theological argument. What follows will attempt to convincingly demonstrate that there is indeed an indication within the New Testament records that, near the end of the first generation of believers, miracles performed by individuals at will were not as numerous as they had been at the birth of the Church, if not completely quiescent.

Understanding the Silence of the Epistles

One of the difficulties in arguing for a decline in miracles or miracle workers from the New Testament record is the silence of so many of the epistles concerning miracles. To say from their silence alone that miracle workers ceased is a weak argument at best. Yet their silence must be taken into account related to the evidence of the rest of the New Testament record. When placed into focus with other elements, this silence becomes additional evidence, strengthening the argument, though alone, it has little or no value.

Those holding to a cessation of miracles must explain if the silence indicates, rather than a decline, simply a lack of interest in them on the part of the apostles. That God intervened in miraculous ways during those days cannot be doubted. Peter's raising of Dorcas in Acts 9:36-43 and Paul's healing of everyone brought to him on Malta in Acts 28:7-10 demonstrates that the apostles were active miracle workers at those points in their ministries. Non-apostles, such as Philip, also performed miracles in the early years of the church as the gospel made its initial penetration into the world (Acts 8:4-8). With this in view, the silence in the epistles, at the least, indicates the relative unimportance of miracles to the Christian's walk and ministry. An even stronger indication of their relative unimportance is the lack of instruction or command regarding their expected presence or governance within the body of Christ.

The debate concerning miracles is made possible by the subject's minimum attention within the New Testament literature, especially the epistles. Neither position can claim any direct Scriptural statement pertaining to their continuance or decline. Both positions interpret the silence as favorable to their view.[45] Hamblin states the problem well when he says, "There is neither any evidence in Acts to suggest that the miracles were to be continued beyond the apostolic age nor to suggest that they would cease."[46] Sterrett repeats the same: "It seems to us that the Scripture nowhere clearly teaches that miraculous manifestations were to cease finally and completely with the apostolic age, nor does it teach that they were to continue throughout the church age in the same way they appeared at the beginning."[47] Some understand this same silence to indicate within itself that miracles were in decline. Sywulka says, "Miracles appear to decrease in importance even within the apostolic age. Their prominence in Acts is notably missing in the epistles."[48] The weakness of this argument, by the way, is the fact that many of these "silent" epistles were written during the time Peter and Paul were performing miracles. Thus, the epistles' silence more likely indicates a lack of significance for miracles and *not* proof of their cessation.

The Place of Paul's Friends in the Argument
Timothy, Epaphroditus, and Trophimus

The illnesses of Timothy, Epaphroditus, and Trophimus play a significant role in the argument for Paul's loss of miracle-working power in the latter part of his ministry. Demonstrating this is critical in any claim of a first-century decline. Habershon's rejection of modern miracle workers is based on his understanding

---

45 Taylor, "Miracles—Yes or No?" 9.
46 Robert L. Hamblin, "Miracles in the Book of Acts," *Southwest Journal of Theology* 17: 1 (Fall 1974): 34.
47 T. Norton Sterrett, "New Testament Charismata" (ThD dissertation, DTS, 1947), 203-204.
48 Sywulka, "Contribution of Hebrews 2:3-4," 12.

of their place in Paul's ministry. She writes, "There is no doubt that the Apostles had power to work miracles in the opening days of the dispensation; but there is no evidence to show that even they continued to possess the power after the final turning away of Israel. On the contrary, there are many indications that the miracles ceased after the close of the Acts. The Apostle Paul could not heal Epaphroditus, Timothy, or Trophimus; nor was his own 'thorn in the flesh' removed."[49] If Paul's failure to heal can be shown to indicate inability, the claim that miracles ceased or declined will be more than merely a theological assertion or an argument from silence. However, their place must be seen in relation to the book of Hebrews and Paul's later epistles, which are otherwise silent concerning miracles.

Possible Explanations for Their Non-healings

First, it might be argued that healing miracles were only for the benefit of unbelievers. The non-healing of Paul and his three associates, at least on initial examination, might argue for such a conclusion. Yet there is other evidence in Scripture to demonstrate that such was not the case during apostolic times, nor was this the reason for their continued illnesses. Second, the vast majority of healings were performed among unevangelized groups of people. If this is interpreted to indicate that the healings were strictly signs accompanying the gospel, it will provide a reason for Paul's inability to heal his three friends. These arguments are damaged, if not destroyed, by the records of Peter raising Dorcas, Paul raising Eutychus, and the mention of healings in the Corinthian church. Third, seeing the "gifts" of healing as separate manifestations of God's presence rather than a permanently lodged gift within an individual would allow an explanation for Paul's inability because Paul was not in a healing phase at those times or that he was not granted gifts for their benefit. This is

---

[49] Habershon, Study of the Miracles, 240.

repudiated by Paul's claims in 2 Corinthians 12:12 and Romans 15:18-19 and the evidence of Acts. Luke's failure to describe healings on certain portions of the journeys, and the second missionary journey altogether, does not mean Paul was inactive. His massive and long-distance healings in Ephesus were described as unique. But his healing everyone who came to him on Malta was not presented as unusual.

2

The Debate

About Modern Faith Healing

Modern Claims of Healing Miracles

Miraculous healings do take place today. To say otherwise would be to limit God's involvement in the lives of His children. People pray for healing. God answers prayer. We should expect Him to heal, sometimes in ways that can only be described as miraculous.

In his two-volume work, *Miracles: The Credibility of the New Testament Accounts*, Craig Keener argues for the present-day experience of miracles within the church. He is very honest in his anecdotal information from interviewing people who believe they are eyewitnesses of miracles in third-world countries. In his analysis, he recognizes the limitations of his research and expertise to evaluate their claims.[50] Keener recounts examples of healing claims and argues that the sheer volume of claims must include valid experiences, even if some miraculous claims can be disproven.[51] He uses this anecdotal evidence from reports of miraculous healings around the world as evidence that healings

---

50 Keener, *Miracles*, 1:266-67.
51 Ibid., 1:506-507.

could have occurred in the first-century Church. His examples span 94 pages (264-358) in three chapters and note the similarity to New Testament reports of Jesus' healings as well as His disciples.[52] All this being said, we should note that he uses terminology that reveals his position is not neutral, either about miracles or toward cessationists. For example, he describes the cessationists as conceding to "deism." He also accuses modern "fundamentalism" of finding a "common cause" with "modernism."[53] Keener sees the attitude of cessationists resulting from "the Reformer's antisupernaturalism" which was a reaction to the Catholic Church's miracle claim. He says that "early Protestants sought to discredit medieval miracles for the most part wholesale; while critical inquiry might have proved more helpful." He then argues that "the majority of Christian scholars" today assume "that God stopped healing people at the close of the first century."[54] So he appears to connect the modern response to the historical roots of the Reformers. While I disagree with him, his candor is appreciated. However, no reader should accept what any author says without evaluating it thoroughly and understanding their presuppositions and purpose in writing, including this author.

Keener is also candidly circumspect about modern faith healers. On the one hand, he defends some based on their theology and claims. On the other, he acknowledges that not everything that happens at healing services is either verifiable or genuine. He notes: "Healing claims on a popular level are hardly limited to specific, known figures, and most of these figures themselves attribute the healings directly to God and (often) to the seeker's faith, rather than to themselves. One could thus fairly readily attribute the healings to such factors rather than specifically to

---

52 Ibid., 1:358.
53 Ibid., 1:376.
54 Ibid., 1:374.

the individuals who most often report them. Claims at public meetings also differ from reports verified subsequently, and I do not work from the assumption that such meetings provide the context of the majority of genuine cases."[55] Further, he notes that "they pray for whoever is in need, but God sovereignly chooses whom and when to heal. This emphasis is faithful to Vineyard teaching and is held among many who pray for the healing of sick persons."[56] However, this can be said of "fundamentalist" and "cessationist" churches as well. Having grown up in fundamentalist and cessationist churches and continued attending similar churches to this day, a year never goes by that I do not hear pastors and lay members ask God to intervene miraculously in healing sick and dying members. I can also say that I have seen God heal in answer to some of those prayers. So miraculous healings are not limited to, nor excluded from any one denomination or church group.

Keener further acknowledges the problem of the power of suggestion and rejects crediting the results to miracles. "Some convinced persons exercise what they believe is faith, but what some psychologists would consider denial. They act as though their symptoms do not exist when no medical change has occurred. While hope and the power of suggestion can exert a positive curative influence in many cases, as doctors also observe, this influence does not prove supernatural intervention. Suggestion can be effective even when the healing practitioner uses deception."[57]

So, what is the issue that is best addressed? It is not a question of miracles but of miracle workers.

---

55 Ibid., 1:403.
56 Ibid., 1:487.
57 Ibid., 2:610.

APOSTOLIC *Signs and Gifts* OF THE SPIRIT

The Issue: Miracle Workers, Not Miracles

It is not the intent of this book to question the continued occurrence of miraculous interventions by God. Today, as since the beginning of time, God has answered the prayers of His saints in miraculous as well as non-miraculous ways. When the question of miracle workers is raised, it is not a question of God's ability or His activity. It is a question of His method. For example, we look at Old Testament saints through whom God worked. Moses was a miracle worker, as were Elijah and Elisha. However, as significant as Noah and Abraham were, neither worked miracles. I'm sure Noah wished he could. It would have saved him decades of ark construction! God accomplished significant things through them but acted through natural means involving divine enablement. It was God who sealed the door of the ark. It was God who enabled Sarah to conceive. However, Sarah's conception was "natural" while Mary's was supernatural. Mary was not a miracle worker, and a miracle worker did not come to cause her pregnancy. God intervened directly in His supernatural enablement and accomplishment. Today we can expect God to do the same, though not as often as is being claimed. One caveat needs to be given here. We probably do see God intervening more often today than in the first few centuries of the church simply because more Christians are praying for His intervention today. So, assuming His interventions are at the same proportion as in the past (same per 1000 requests), we would expect many more simply from the growing numbers of saints petitioning Him and interceding for one another. James's statement that we have not because we ask not has the corollary that the more often we ask God to intervene, we can expect to see Him do so (Jas 4:2).

The apostles provide an example of the difference between miracle workers and those who simply pray for God's intervention. They went from being non-miracle workers to miracle workers to non-miracle workers and then back to miracle workers. When they met Jesus and became His followers, none had any supernatural abilities. None performed miracles, even as they followed Jesus and witnessed His miracles. Then they were commissioned by Jesus to go in pairs to the nation of Israel with the gospel message, "Repent, for the kingdom of Heaven is at hand!" (Matt 10:5-8). Jesus granted them the authority to heal the sick, raise the dead, and cast out demons. This they did at will and without fail. Following this period, they apparently lost the ability, as was evident with the moonstruck (epileptic) boy in Matthew 17:17-21. Their surprise at their inability to cast the demon out is noteworthy. They expected the demon to come out at their command. They had not realized that the authority they had been given by Jesus earlier was no longer in effect. Jesus did not restore that authority to them but instructed them, and us, to pray and fast, thereby indicating that God would act on such possessions directly. The apostles show no signs of miracle-working ability again until after the day of Pentecost and the birth of the church. Acts 2:43 and 5:12 note that "signs and wonders" were being done by all the apostles. Other non-apostles, such as Stephen (Acts 6:8) and Philip (Acts 8:6-7), did so as well.

Luke focuses on Peter's miraculous activity early in Acts, describing him as healing at will. The first example is when Peter heals the lame man in Acts 3:6-7. This leads to the second sermon and the addition of five thousand Old Testament saints to the body of Christ. Soon after this, as the message of his healing the lame man spreads, people come from miles around, and even his shadow heals people (Acts 5:14-16). Here Luke tells us that of those who came, "all were healed." As time progresses, Peter goes to Lydda and heals Aeneas of his paralysis (Acts 9:32-35) and then raises Dorcas from the dead (Acts 9:36-43).[58] After this, with the transition of Luke's focus from Peter to Paul, Pe-

---

58   Peter's judgments on Ananias and Sapphira (Acts 5:1-11) were "miraculous" exercises of apostolic authority as well. However, it is not mentioned in the main discussion because the focus is on the kinds of miracles we see claimed today.

ter's miracle-working activity is no longer reported but may be assumed to have continued.[59]

Paul exhibits a similar ability to work miracles at will and without fail, even as Peter.[60] Paul heals a lame Gentile at Lystra (Acts 14:8-10).[61] During the Jerusalem Council, he and Barnabas report on their miraculous activities as evidence of God's endorsement of their message and ministry (Acts 15:12).[62] Then, in Ephesus, he performs miracles at will (Acts 19:11). In contrast to Paul's authority are the sons of Sceva who get themselves beat up by demons they attempt to cast out in Jesus' name without His authority (Acts 19:13-16). On his way to Jerusalem, Paul raises Eutychus from the dead (Acts 20:8-12). During his journey to Rome, on Malta, Paul again heals at will, first the father-in-law of his host and then everyone who comes (Acts 28:7-9).

We see from these examples that the apostles and others within the early days of the church had miraculous spiritual gifts and were miracle workers. The authority they received from God enabled them to heal all who came. There were likely others who were, at times, agents of God's supernatural interventions but who could not perform a miracle at will. Yet that leads to the question of today. Do we still have miracle workers who can exhibit the power of God at will, or just occasional miracles when God intervenes in response to prayer?

---

[59] An example of God's miraculous intervention without the use of human agency is the death of Herod when he was struck with worms by an angel for failing to give God His due glory (Acts 12:20-23).

[60] This fits with one of Luke's themes in the book of Acts, that Paul was as much an apostle as Peter. One proof of the legitimacy of Paul's apostleship was his ability to do everything Peter did, and better. He does the same kinds of miracles, including cursing someone (though not killing him, Acts 13:8-12), raising Eutychus from the dead (crushed skull or broken neck, Acts 20:7-12), and healing people indirectly, with Paul's being done from a distance as well and described as "unusual" (Acts 19:11-2).

[61] This might be viewed as literally parallel to Peter's healing of the lame Jewish man in Acts 3. Again, developing Luke's theme of Paul's apostleship.

[62] One might ask why Paul did not heal himself and Silas after their beatings in Philippi. The best answer would be Paul's own words in Col 1:24 that such sufferings "fill up in my flesh what is lacking in the afflictions of Christ, for the sake of His body, which is the church." He chose not to relieve himself of suffering that resulted from persecution for the gospel.

Arguments for Miraculous Healers Today

One of the strongest proponents of miracle-working was the late John Wimber, founder of the Vineyard Movement and whose writings continue to be influential today. He argues that miracle-working was an essential element of Spirit-empowered gospel presentations. He says,

> The church should announce and demonstrate the Kingdom of God. Kingdom evangelism involves power evangelism: that means evangelism that transcends the rational through the demonstration of God's power in signs and wonders and introduces the numinous of God. This involves a presentation of the good news of God's reign accompanied with the manifest presence of God. Power evangelism is spontaneous and is directed by the Holy Spirit. The result is often explosive church growth.[63]

> By power evangelism I mean a presentation of the gospel that is rational but that also transcends the rational. The explanation of the gospel comes with a demonstration of God's power through signs and wonders. Power evangelism is a spontaneous, Spirit-inspired, empowered presentation of the gospel. Power evangelism is evangelism that is preceded and undergirded by supernatural demonstrations of God's presence."[64]

He identifies his understanding of the role of miraculous spiritual gifts in the introduction to his book, *Power Evangelism*.

> Once I accepted the fact that all the spiritual gifts are for today, I found a key for effective evangelism: combining the proclamation with the demonstration of gospel

---

[63] John Wimber, as quoted in *Renewal Journal* #10: Evangelism Renewal: Brisbane. http://www.christiananswers.net/evangelism/methods/powerevangelism.html. Accessed October 10, 2016.
[64] John Wimber, *Power Evangelism* (San Francisco: Harper and Row, 1986) 35.

... Rather than detracting from the proclamation of the gospel, the gifts, I observed, when correctly practiced, open people to a clearer understanding and practice of Christianity. There is unusual power and effectiveness in this form of evangelism, which is why I call it "power evangelism."[65]

It is what he called a "gospel advancer."[66]

Arguments Against Miraculous Healers Today

Many within Evangelicalism reject the legitimacy of those who claim to be miracle workers or agents through whom God acts in miraculous ways.[67] The most notable author would be John MacArthur, whose book, *Charismatic Chaos*, questions the movement's validity concerning its claims to miracles and other teachings.[68] He draws a contrast between the biblical description of miracles and what is seen in the modern healing movement. He argues that where "Jesus and the apostles instantly and completely healed people born blind, a paralytic, a man with a withered arm—all obvious, indisputable miracles ... By contrast, most modern miracles are nearly always partial, gradual, or temporary."[69] The second line of argumentation he uses as evidence of its invalidity is the manner of death for many modern faith healers. These include Hobart Freeman, who died of pneumonia and heart failure. William Branham died of his injuries from a car wreck. A. A. Allen died from sclerosis of the

---

65   Ibid., xx.
66   Wimber, *Power Healing* (San Francisco: Harper and Row, 1987) 42.
67   Additionally, the internet has many sites with arguments against modern faith healers, or articles exposing fraudulent healing claims and activities. Examples would include sites like csicop.org (Center for Scientific Inquiry), evidenceunseen.com, thewordonthewordoffaithinfoblog.com, web.randi.org, quackwatch.org, quora.com, and jesus-is-savior.com, to name a few. Not all sites are Christian or even sympathetic toward Christianity per se. And, though some are dedicated to exposing faith healers, others simply include them in their list of interests.
68   John F. MacArthur, Jr., *Charismatic Chaos* (Grand Rapids: Zondervan, 1992).
69   Ibid., 110.

liver. Kathryn Kuhlman died of heart failure after nearly 20 years of struggle with heart disease. Ruth Carter Stapleton died of cancer.[70] Writing before John Wimber's death, MacArthur notes Wimber's "chronic heart problems."[71] As it turned out, Wimber did not die from heart problems but a brain aneurysm following a fall. Granted, he *had* experienced serious illnesses that were not healed miraculously, including cancer and bypass surgery.[72] However, death by an aneurysm should not be used to discredit him. Even faith healers must die eventually, and they will not die of good health. Even so, MacArthur's best evidence in this respect is those who had chronic problems that led to their deaths and yet could not heal themselves. Yet even this should not be given much weight since the Apostle Paul, who could heal at will, had a chronic health problem, his thorn in the flesh, that he prayed for release from three times. He could not heal himself, and God refused to heal him as well (2 Cor 12:7-10). It must be noted that Paul's infirmity had a purpose, to keep him humble. So one might argue that he would be an exception. However, it still stands that even apostles had health problems. Thus, any faith healer's inability to heal himself does not automatically invalidate his claims.

Another example of arguments used by those denying the validity of modern faith healing is the statement made by Habershon: "There is no doubt that the Apostles had power to work miracles in the opening days of the dispensation; but there is no evidence to show that even they continued to possess the power after the final turning away of Israel. On the contrary, there are many indications that the miracles ceased after the close of the Acts. The Apostle Paul could not heal Epaphroditus, Timothy, or

---

70 Ibid., 195.
71 Ibid.
72 Joe Maxwell, Heather Johnson, John Geary, "Vineyard Founder Wimber Dies," *Christianity Today* Vol. 42, No. 1 (January 12, 1998): 58.

Trophimus; nor was his own 'thorn in the flesh' removed."[73] This same thought is repeated by others such as Ryrie and McCune.[74] Paul's friends' illnesses may provide possible evidence of a decline in miracles but alone produce an inadequate argument. Other questions must be answered regarding the place of these men in the debate. What is their relationship to the historical record and the growth of the church? What were the circumstances of their illnesses? Would those circumstances indicate that Paul would have been more inclined to heal them if he could, rather than leaving sick? Additionally, to claim Paul's non-healing serves as evidence of a loss of miracle-working power completely ignores his own testimony. Bruce takes a more defensible position when he sees Paul's "splinter in the flesh" following his transportation into paradise as a means employed by God for "the furtherance of the divine purpose."[75] He comments concerning Paul's illness: "The sequel to Paul's mystical experience was a distressing, indeed humiliating, physical ailment which he feared at first might be a handicap to his effective ministry but which in fact, by giving his self-esteem a knockout blow and keeping him constantly dependent on the divine enabling, proved to be a help, not a handicap. Many guesses have been made about the identity of this 'splinter in the flesh'; and their variety proved the impossibility of a certain diagnosis .... His thrice repeated prayer for the removal of the ailment was answered, not by his deliverance from it, but by his receiving the necessary grace to bear it—not simply to live with it but to be thankful for it."

Further, 2 Corinthians 12:7-10 was written at the same time as 12:12 in which Paul was still pointing to his own working of miracles as present proof of his apostleship. It was written when, according to the record of Acts, Paul was clearly capable of and

---

73 Habershon, *Study of the Miracles*, 240.
74 McCune, "A Biblical Study of Tongues and Miracles," 19; Ryrie, "Greater Works Than These," 34.
75 F. F. Bruce, *Paul: Apostle of the Heart Set Free* (Grand Rapids: William B. Eerdmans, 1977), 227.

continuing to work miraculous healings at will. His explanation that the thorn in the flesh was given to him permanently to keep him humble provides the basis for understanding his non-healing. While unable to help himself, he could still heal others. Thus, to point to Paul's non-healing as proof of a lack of ability does not find support in Scripture and is easily discredited. Instead, his condition indicates that healing authority was still dependent on God's will and His direction for its expression.

It may also be argued, though not convincingly, that Paul's failure to heal other believers or himself implies that believers were not to expect healing from God. [76] MacArthur, believing that Paul had miracle power until his death, argues that "the purpose of the gift of healing was not to keep Christians healthy." Rather, it was a "sign to unbelievers."[77] The weakness of this position is that Paul very willingly healed Eutychus, raising him from the dead at a time when there were no unbelievers present for whom the miracle would be a sign (since they had met to have fellowship). Though a resurrection is undoubtedly a miracle of a different caliber from simply restoring one's diseased body, it still involves restoration.

Further, the Corinthians' gifts of healing certainly benefited believers since they were given for the common good of the body of Christ. Even so, God's refusal to heal Paul requires that his friends' non-healings be examined and the question of purpose be asked concerning them. Were they similarly touched by God and expected to suffer according to His will? Or were their illnesses of a different sort? This is especially significant with Timothy, who had a chronic intestinal illness rather than some acute condition such as Epaphroditus and Trophimus faced. This issue is addressed further below.

---

76   Don W. Hillis, *Tongues, Healing, and You!* (Grand Rapids: Baker Book House, 1969), 27.
77   John F. MacArthur, Jr., *The Charismatics* (Grand Rapids: Zondervan, 1978), 149.

The Place of Faith in God's Miraculous Acts

What role does faith play in God's divine interventions? Does our faith limit Him? Would this explain the failure of modern faith healers to heal a hundred percent of those who come to them? A quick scan of the internet reveals a common theme that the person's faith is key to receiving healing or some other miracle from God.[78] This has historically been found in books written by ministers engaged in healing ministries.[79] Ken Blue identified this doctrine as " 'faith formula' thinking" in which "there is a strict causality between faith and healing. It holds that all divine blessings, such as health and prosperity, are constantly and fully available to all Christians. These benefits, which are supposedly available to every and any child of God, may be instantly appropriated, provided the individual Christian knows enough and believes enough."[80] Dale A. Robins expresses it well. "Don't stop praying and believing! This is the most common reason why some people don't receive healing. They get discouraged and give up their faith."[81] But what do we see in Scripture, especially the ministry of Jesus?

---

[78] Michael Bradley, "Having Faith and Belief That God Can Actually Heal You," www.bible-knowledge.com/faith-god-can-heal-you. Accessed November 29, 2018; Gloria Copeland, "Take Your Healing – By Faith," www.hopefaithprayer.com/take-healing-faith-gloria-copeland. Accessed November 29, 2018; Marcia Greenwood, "Faith and Healing," www.tgm.org/faithmp.htm, accessed November 29, 2018; Kenneth E. Hagin, "Faith Brings Results," www.rhema.org/index.php?option =comcontent&view=article &id=1026:faith-brings-esults&-catid=46&Itemid=141. Accessed November 29, 2018. Larry Keefauver ("Is Your Healing Contingent on Your Faith?" Charisma Magazine, 10 a.m. EST, 12/4/2012, www.charismamag.com/spirit/supernatural/4537-the-myths-of-faith-healing. Accessed November 29, 2018) shows a more balanced view, while still asserting the need for faith in the believer. He says, "Our faith helps us receive healing, just as the lack of faith hinders healing. But healing does not depend on faith. Healing depends on the Healer."

[79] Emily Gardiner Neal, *The Healing Power of Christ*, New York: Hawthorn Books, 1972. Oral Roberts (*Exactly How You May Receive Your Healing Through Faith* [Tulsa, OK: Oral Roberts, 1958], 9) writes, "What God can do for us is significant only as we believe he will do these things for us. The truth is that Jesus, who came to earth to show us what God is like, proved that what God can do for us, he will do, if we conform to his will and believe."

[80] Ken Blue, *Authority to Heal* (Downers Grove, IL: InterVarsity Press, 1987), 42.

[81] Dale A. Robbins, "Healing is One of God's Benefits," *Victorious Publications*, Grass Valley, CA – Nashville. www.victorious.org/pub/receive-healing-116. Accessed November 29, 2018.

Jesus' Limited Ministry in Nazareth

When Jesus visited His hometown of Nazareth, we are told that "He did not do many mighty works there because of their unbelief." At first glance, one might think that their unbelief led to Jesus' inability to do miracles. Rather, it led to a lack of *opportunities* to do miracles. Thus, Louis Barbieri correctly notes the "result" of their lack of faith was that Jesus "performed few miracles" in Nazareth.[82] In this case, the lack of faith was not that they did not believe Jesus could do the miracles. They knew He could and had been doing them in their own town. Instead, it was the unbelief that resulted from their rejection of Him and offense at His messianic claims.[83] It was their failure to come that limited Jesus.[84] However, it must also be noted that Matthew did not say Jesus failed to do *any* miracles but that He did not do *many*. Thus, as John Noland observes, "Jesus' miracle-working power was still evident" ... even "in the face of unbelief."[85] Though not a teaching point of Matthew, Donald Hagner observes well that Jesus, by practice, did not "perform miracles in order to counter-

---

[82] Louis A. Barbieri, Jr., "Matthew," in *The Bible Knowledge Commentary: An Exposition of the Scriptures*, ed. J. F. Walvoord and R. B. Zuck, vol. 2 (Wheaton, IL: Victor Books, 1985), 53; Leon Morris, *The Gospel according to Matthew*, The Pillar New Testament Commentary (Grand Rapids: William B. Eerdmans, 1992), 367.

[83] Craig Blomberg, *Matthew*, The New American Commentary, vol. 22 (Nashville: Broadman & Holman, 1992), 229. Reflecting on this passage, Lenski (R. C. H. Lenski, *The Interpretation of St. Matthew's Gospel* [Minneapolis, MN: Augsburg Publishing House, 1961], 553-54) observes, "It has become traditional to assume that faith precedes every miracle although this tradition is disregarded every time a miracle is wrought where faith is plainly not present (as for instance in 8:28, etc.). How unbelief prevented the performance of many miracles is shown in Luke 4:28-38. The people of Nazareth rose up, thrust Jesus out of the city, and tried to kill him.

[84] William Hendriksen and Simon J. Kistemaker, *Exposition of the Gospel according to Matthew*, New Testament Commentary, vol. 9 (Grand Rapids: Baker Book House, 1953-2001), 582; Charles F. Pfeiffer and Everett Falconer Harrison, eds., *The Wycliffe Bible Commentary: New Testament* (Chicago: Moody Press, 1962), Matt 13:54; A.T. Robertson, *Word Pictures in the New Testament* (Nashville: Broadman Press, 1933), Matt 13:58; Stuart K. Weber, *Matthew*, Holman New Testament Commentary, vol. 1 (Nashville: Broadman & Holman, 2000), 206.

[85] John Nolland, "Preface," in *The Gospel of Matthew: A Commentary on the Greek Text*, New International Greek Testament Commentary (Grand Rapids: William B. Eerdmans; 2005), 577.

act unbelief."[86] Rather, He did them out of compassion and, most often, in response to the recipient's request.

Jesus Healed Without Faith Exercised by the Beneficiary

John's Gospel contains an example of someone healed by Jesus apart from faith. We see this in his treatment of the man at the Pool of Bethesda in John 5. As will be seen below, the man does not demonstrate faith in Jesus before or after the miracle. Yet Jesus heals him, nonetheless.

As background, this account appears to be included by John for two reasons. First, it is part of the development of his theme on Jesus' omniscience, which is a sub-theme of Jesus' deity. This theme is introduced in the first chapter of his Gospel with Jesus' awareness of Nathaniel's whereabouts (John 1:48). In John 2:24-25, we are then told that Jesus "knew all *men*, and had no need that anyone should testify of man, for He knew what was in man."[87] This followed John's statement, a play on words, that while many "believed" (*episteusan*, ἐπίστευσαν) in Jesus, He was not "believing" in them (*ouk episteuen auton autois*, οὐκ ἐπίστευεν αὐτὸν αὐτοῖς). This is translated as "commit Himself to them," or something similar in most English translations, and misses the play-on-words intended by John.[88] John follows his statement with four examples of people that Jesus knows what is in them. He then completes this theme in chapter 6 with a crowd that Jesus knows does not believe in Him (John 6:64). Nicodemus serves as an example of a believer Jesus knows He cannot trust because he is one of the leaders who fear men more than

---

86 Donald A. Hagner, *Matthew 1–13*, Word Biblical Commentary, vol. 33A (Dallas: Word, Inc., 1998), 406. Lange and Schaff concur (John Peter Lange and Philip Schaff, *A Commentary on the Holy Scriptures: Matthew* [Bellingham, WA: Logos Bible Software, 2008], 255) and say, "He found them not prepared to receive, and therefore would not as He could not. The latter expression indicates not a want of power, but the moral limits which Himself imposed on the exercise of His power. However, it also implies that we are not to regard these displays of Christ's power as merely the manifestations of absolute might."

87 *The New King James Version* (Nashville: Thomas Nelson, 1982), John 2:24–25.

88 *The New Century Version* breaks from the pattern and translates it as "Jesus did not believe in them" and thereby captures the play-on-words intended by John.

the approval of God (John 3:1-15; 12:42-43). The woman at the well is an unbeliever that Jesus knows will believe in Him and testify of Him to her community (John 4:1-26). The royal official is an example of a believer Jesus knows will believe Him and act on His word (John 4:46-54). Then John provides the example of an unbeliever that Jesus knows will continue in his unbelief and will betray Him, the man at the Pool of Bethesda (John 5:1-16). Jesus heals the man knowing his sinful past and that his illness is sin-related, thus His warning about worse happening if he continues in sin (John 5:14). He later identifies Himself to the man so that the healed man can report Him to the Jewish authorities, who then responded by persecuting and challenging Jesus. This leads to John's second reason for including the account, which was to set the stage for Jesus' discussion with the Jews about His authority and to develop John's theme of Jesus' deity (John 5:17-47).

How do we know that Jesus healed the man apart from faith? First, this is the only healing where faith is not mentioned even once, and so it is unique to John's accounts. Its absence is significant in light of John's emphasis on believing throughout the Gospel. Second, the man's response to Jesus' question was to talk about his problems, not to ask for help.[89] Andreas Köstenberger notes well that even after Jesus' question, his "response makes clear that he could not see past the water as his healing agent."[90] Third, unlike the account of the royal official just before him, we

---

89 Kenneth O. Gangel, *John*, Holman New Testament Commentary, vol. 4 (Nashville: Broadman & Holman, 2000), 97; Donald Guthrie, "John," in *New Bible Commentary: 21st Century Edition*, ed. D. A. Carson *et al.*, 4th ed. (Downers Grove, IL: Inter-Varsity Press, 1994), 1036.

90 Andreas J. Köstenberger, *John*, Baker Exegetical Commentary on the New Testament (Grand Rapids: Baker Academic, 2004), 180. Gerald L. Borchert (*John 1–11*, The New American Commentary, vol. 25A [Nashville: Broadman & Holman, 1996], 232) notes well, "The only hope evident in his testimony was his commitment to a myth of a periodic miraculous troubling of the pool, which allegedly brought healing to the first person able to jump in." Andrew T. Lincoln (*The Gospel according to Saint John*, Black's New Testament Commentary [London: Continuum, 2005], 194) in a way defends him when he notes, "The man's response can be read as his treating Jesus' question as an offer of help to get him into the pool rather than as an offer of direct healing." However, in response to each of these interpreters, the invalid did not ask Jesus to help him in. He just complained.

are not told that after his healing, he "believed" in Jesus. Rather, John tells us he left the pool without knowing Jesus, which would indicate that he did not even try to find out.[91] When asked by the Jews, he has no idea who had healed him and has to be sought out by Jesus, who then identifies Himself. His response is not that of the Samaritan leper who glorifies God and thanks Jesus (Luke 17:11-19). Nor is it like the man born blind in John's Gospel, who worships Jesus (John 9:38). Instead, as soon as he knows who his healer is, he reports Jesus to the authorities as a violator of the Sabbath. This is not the action of faith but a picture of betrayal, an act of unbelief and lack of gratitude.[92]

So then, how was he healed? Jesus' command healed him instantly and apart from faith.[93] Merrill Tenney observes well, "The healing was not a response to a request, nor did it presuppose an expression of faith on the part of the man."[94] Further, Hendrickson and Kistemaker note John's use of "immediately" (*eutheōs*, εὐθέως) emphasizes how suddenly he was healed following those many years of illness. "*This* recovery is neither gradual nor partial; nor, we may well add, was the sickness faked (as some, nevertheless, have supposed)."[95]

---

91   George R. Beasley-Murray, *John*, Word Biblical Commentary, vol. 36 (Dallas: Word, Inc., 2002), 74.

92   Lenski (*St. Matthew's Gospel*, 363) says, "Here is a plain instance where the miracle precedes the faith, where the faith even follows some time later." Lewis Foster (*John: Unlocking the Scriptures for You*, Standard Bible Studies [Cincinnati, OH: Standard, 1987], 59) agrees with him and says, "By that command, the man was challenged to put his trust in Jesus. He did so, and he was healed. In fact, Jesus issued a whole series of challenges when He told the man to pick up his mat and walk." I disagree with both. The man's betrayal of Jesus would indicate that faith never followed. Rather this is a good example that miracles, even those received, do not in and of themselves engender faith in their recipients.

93   Edwin A. Blum, "John" in *The Bible Knowledge Commentary: An Exposition of the Scriptures*, ed. J. F. Walvoord and R. B. Zuck, vol. 2 (Wheaton, IL: Victor Books, 1985), 289.

94   Merrill C. Tenney, *John*, The Expositor's Bible Commentary, vol. 9 (Grand Rapids: Zondervan, 1981), 62.

95   Hendriksen and Kistemaker, *Matthew*, 193.

Jesus Raised the Dead When No One Else Expected It

Two instances of resurrections by Jesus did not require faith from those witnessing it, much less the ones receiving it. These involved Jesus restoring the life of a widow's son and a beloved brother.

The raising of the widow's son at Nain is an excellent example of Jesus' miraculous ministry that resulted from His compassion rather than the faith of its beneficiaries (Luke 7:11-16).[96] As Jesus enters the village and sees the funeral procession, He feels compassion for the widow for whom this is her only son and, therefore, her only hope of help in her old age. Luke's description indicates that no one expects Jesus to do what He does, neither the widow nor casket bearers, not even His disciples. There is no indication that anyone recognizes Him. It is Jesus who takes the initiative. If Jesus had not touched the casket, its bearers would have walked past Him and laid the young man in the ground. Speaking words of comfort to the mother, Jesus did not wait for an expression of faith but immediately restored the young man's life.[97]

The raising of Lazarus reflects the same power of Jesus to heal or raise the dead, apart from anyone's faith, whether it is a lack of faith caused by unbelief or a lack of expectation (John 11). That no one expects Jesus to raise Lazarus is evident from His conversations with the disciples as well as Martha and Mary. After delaying for three days, Jesus tells the disciples He intends to return to Judea and "wake" Lazarus up. They balk at the idea, missing Jesus' figurative use of "sleep" to indicate death (John 11:13-14). When Jesus clarifies that Lazarus is dead and He is going to "wake him up," rather than realizing the significance of what Jesus has just said, Thomas replies with, "Let us go that

---

96 Darrell L. Bock, Luke: 1:1–9:50, Baker Exegetical Commentary on the New Testament, vol. 1 (Grand Rapids, MI: Baker Academic, 1994), 650; I. Howard Marshall, The Gospel of Luke: A Commentary on the Greek Text, New International Greek Testament Commentary (Exeter: Paternoster Press, 1978), 285-86.

97 Hendriksen and Kistemaker, *Matthew*, 385.

we may die with him" (John 11:16). This is undoubtedly a statement of loyalty, even if sarcastically spoken, but not of expectation. At this point, I would not accuse Thomas of a lack of faith. John does not appear to be indicating that. Rather, the disciples are more concerned with the danger of returning than with the significance of what is about to happen. With Jesus' arrival, we have two conversations by Martha and then Mary that indicate neither sister expects Jesus to raise Lazarus from death. In fact, both chide Him for not being there when Lazarus needed His help and was still living. The indication is that they believed Jesus would have healed Lazarus if He had gotten back in time, but not that He would raise him from the dead. Even when He promises Martha that Lazarus will rise again, she dismisses the possibility of Jesus raising him by acknowledging her belief in a future resurrection of the dead on the "last day" (John 11:24). Then, when Jesus responds to her, "I am the resurrection and the life. He who believes in Me, though he may die, he shall live. And whoever lives and believes in Me shall never die. Do you believe this?" (John 11:24-26), her answer indicates that she is still not expecting Jesus to raise her brother. Instead of addressing resurrection, she simply affirms her belief that Jesus is her Messiah, thus, "Yes, Lord, I believe that You are the Christ, the Son of God, who is to come into the world."[98] This may be the result of a Jewish belief that, when a person died, their spirit hovered near their body for the first three days and then departed on the fourth. At that point, they were irretrievably dead.[99]

---

98 *The New King James Version* (Nashville: Thomas Nelson, 1982), John 11:25–27.
99 Robert B. Hughes and J. Carl Laney, *Tyndale Concise Bible Commentary*, The Tyndale Reference Library (Wheaton, IL: Tyndale House, 2001), 476; Andrew Paterson, *Opening Up John's Gospel*, Opening Up Commentary (Leominster: Day One Publications, 2010), 91-92; H. L. Willmington, *Willmington's Bible Handbook* (Wheaton, IL: Tyndale House, 1997), 616. D. A. Carson (*The Gospel according to John*, The Pillar New Testament Commentary [Grand Rapids: William B. Eerdmans, 1991], 411) says, "From a slightly later date there are sources attesting the rabbinic belief that the soul hovers over the body of the deceased person for the first three days, 'intending to re-enter it, but as soon as it sees its appearance change', *i.e.* that decomposition has set in, it departs (Leviticus Rabbah [a rabbinical commentary] 18:1 [on Lv. 15:1]; for other references *cf.* SB 2. 544f.). At that point death is irreversible."

Jesus chose to raise Lazarus on the fourth day so that no one could miss the significance of His life-giving act. By the fourth day, Jesus would have to do more than return the spirit to its body. He would have to reverse the decay process that would be in full effect. It may also be that Mary and Martha would have given up on any chance of resurrection for this reason. Even so, Jesus' purpose is not hindered by anyone's misunderstanding and, therefore, their lack of expectation or faith. He raises Lazarus to everybody's amazement.[100]

This is a good place to pause and discuss how people responded to Jesus' miracles and the place of miracles today as it relates to faith. Do miracles produce faith in those who witness them? We saw with the man at the Pool of Bethesda that even the recipient of a miracle might still not believe in Jesus. When Jesus raised Lazarus from the dead, not everybody witnessing the miracle believed in Him. When He fed the five thousand, the majority of them failed to believe in Him and walked away from Him the day following the miracle. However, this is a teaching championed by John Wimber that continues to be taught today. As noted earlier, he asserts that kingdom evangelism, or "power evangelism," involves the presentation of the gospel accompanied by "the manifest presence of God" through signs and wonders.[101]

---

100 I have always been amazed at the shortest verse in the Bible, "Jesus wept." As I have puzzled over its significance over the years, I began wondering how it is that He would weep while knowing that Lazarus was about to be alive again and everyone's grief would be dispelled by joy. Common answers for Jesus' tears include anger at death (Köstenberger, *John*, 339; Robert Jamieson, A. R. Fausset, and David Brown, *Commentary Critical and Explanatory on the Whole Bible*, vol. 2 [Oak Harbor, WA: Logos Research Systems, Inc., 1997], 150), sorrow over the effects of sin and death (Blum, "John," 314; Beasley-Murray, *John*, 193), grieving over the unbelief of those around Him (Carson, *John*, 416), or "the failure of his followers to recognize his mission as the agent of God. God's Son was in their midst" (Borchert, *John 1–11*, 360). A better answer seems to be that Jesus, even knowing Lazarus was about to return to life, could not stand among those He loved without feeling the pain and sorrow they were experiencing. Jesus wept *with* them. He was one with them in sorrow. When we grieve over a loved one who has died, we do not grieve alone. God grieves with us, even as He rejoices with that loved one who is now with Him in heaven. That is the depth of God's love for each of us, a love that continues into eternity. A love felt by God more deeply than we can feel. A love that moves God to emotions far more intense than we can know.

101 John Wimber as quoted in *Renewal Journal* #10: Evangelism Renewal: Brisbane. Accessed Oct 10, 2016 at www.christiananswers.net/evangelism/methods/powerevangelism.html.

Yet the testimony of Scripture seems to indicate that miracles were not a powerful evangelistic tool, even when performed by Jesus. There were two responses to Jesus' raising of Lazarus.[102] Some believed, while others continued in unbelief and went back and reported Jesus to the Sanhedrin.[103] Some have argued that those who reported Jesus to the Sanhedrin were also believers. For example, Lenski argues that "some of them" in John 11:45 "means a few of those ... who believed" and who reported to the Pharisees what He had done, but not to denounce Jesus. Rather, "in all good faith and with all sincerity ... they went in order to convince these opponents of Jesus that they were surely wrong in their opinion about him."[104] However, John's grammar indicates otherwise. Lange and Schaff describe them better as "agents or spies for the Pharisees" rather than seekers who would come to faith. They say further that "the hardened denunciators held the same opinion to which Caiaphas gives utterance [sic] ver. 50, and considered Jesus to be merely a dangerous man."[105] William McDonald explains well the problem of eye witnesses not believing. He says that "the effect of a miracle on a person's life depends on his moral condition. If one's heart is evil, rebellious, and unbelieving, he will not believe even though he were to see one raised from the dead. That was the case here. Some of the Jews who witnessed the miracle were unwilling to accept the Lord Jesus as their Messiah in spite of such undeniable proof."[106] So why would the Pharisees not believe? Donald Guthrie notes well that this climactic sign of Jesus did not change the hearts of the Pharisees. Rather than debating the validity of the miracle, they expressed deep concern for its impact on others. As Guthrie

---

102 Blum, "John," 315; Beasley-Murray, *John*, 196.
103 Borchert, *John 1–11*, 363; Carson, *John*, 419; Hughes and Laney, *Concise Bible Commentary*, 476; Pfeiffer and Harrison, *Wycliffe Bible Commentary: New Testament*, John 11:45.
104 Lenski, St. John's Gospel, 821.
105 Lange and Schaff, Matthew, 362.
106 William MacDonald, Believer's Bible Commentary: Old and New Testaments, ed. Arthur Farstad (Nashville: Thomas Nelson, 1995), 1534. Bold (emphasis) his.

states well that "their fear was that everyone (i.e., except themselves) would believe in Jesus."[107]

Christ Sustained Faith

It seems appropriate to pause and examine the raising of Jairus' daughter at this time (Mark 5:21-43). In contrast to the raising of Lazarus, she has only been dead a short time. Where Jesus purposefully delays returning to Judea to raise Lazarus, He responds immediately to the father's request. Further, her parents have exercised faith in Jesus, at least while they know she lives.[108] We see this in the father's request, "Come and lay Your hands on her, that she may be healed, and she will live." Thus, we might conclude that he is thinking of Jesus as a healer and not a life-giver.

Nonetheless, his request expresses faith, to which Jesus responds. Before they reach Jairus' home, the story is interrupted by the woman with the incurable flow of blood whose healing comes without Jesus' direct intervention. This would surely strengthen the father's faith and increase his hope, even as he anxiously awaits Jesus' completion of His conversation with the woman and return to walking to his house. When the news comes that his daughter has died, Jesus calls on him not to fear and to keep believing. James Brooks says well, "The best explanation is that Jesus overheard what the messengers said and accepted the reality of the child's death but that he refused to accept the finality of death. Though he did not tell the ruler how the crisis would end, Jesus urged him to believe that all would end well. In any event, the necessity of faith is emphasized."[109] As Lenski notes, both commands are present imperatives, whose

---

107 Guthrie, "John," 1050. Italics his.
108 Paul R. McReynolds, Mark: Unlocking the Scriptures for You, Standard Bible Studies (Cincinnati, OH: Standard, 1989), 55.
109 James A. Brooks, Mark, The New American Commentary, vol. 23 (Nashville: Broadman & Holman, 1991), 94.

durative force implies he has been trusting Jesus and needs to continue to do so.[110] James Edwards fleshes this idea out. "The present tense of the Greek imperative means to *keep* believing, to hold onto faith rather than give in to despair. With respect to his daughter's circumstances, Jairus's future is closed; but with respect to Jesus, it is still open. Faith is not something *Jairus* has but something that has *Jairus*, carrying him from despair to hope. Jesus' authoritative word to Jairus is not to fear but to believe."[111] Thus, Jesus affirms his faith. Jairus's faith can be seen in his allowing Jesus to continue going to his house even after the messengers tell him his daughter has died.[112] When He responds to their news with assuring words, Jairus apparently responds to Jesus and expresses faith.[113]

Mourning is already in progress when Jesus enters Jairus's home. Jesus' rebuke of the mourners and statement that the child only sleeps is met with ridicule from the mourners, who Jesus subsequently expels from the house. Then, with only the parents and His inner circle of disciples, Jesus restores her to life. Luke (8:55) tells us that when Jesus takes her by the hand and commands her to arise, her "spirit returned to her." This indicates that Jesus' reference to her being "asleep" is the same as Lazarus. Her death is temporary, and Jesus, who is the resurrection and the life (John 11:25), is about to "awaken" her.

Mark tells us that those present with Jesus "were amazed" at the miracle. Luke (8:56) tells us her parents were astonished. This, again, indicates that none of them, including the disciples,

---

110 R. C. H. Lenski, The Interpretation of St. Mark's Gospel (Minneapolis: Augsburg, 1961), 228.

111 James R. Edwards, *The Gospel according to Mark*, The Pillar New Testament Commentary (Grand Rapids: William B. Eerdmans, 2002), 166. Italics his.

112 Walter W. Wessel, *Mark*, The Expositor's Bible Commentary (Grand Rapids: Zondervan, 1984), 662.

113 Robert A. Guelich, *Mark 1–8:26*, Word Biblical Commentary, vol. 34A (Dallas: Word, Inc., 1998), 300.

expected Jesus to raise the girl from the dead.[114] However, Jesus' words must have sustained the father's faith enough for him to continue relying on Jesus rather than giving up hope.

God Responds to Faith Today as Then (James 5:13-18)

A discussion of miracle workers, especially faith healers, cannot be complete without addressing the issue of the commands and promise of James 5:13-18 as it relates to the one praying.[115] In this passage, James raises the issue of his readers' physical and emotional state, and so of us. What he writes is not limited to the church of his day but applies equally to us today. God does still intervene on behalf of His children in accordance with His promise in James. However, many who claim these verses do not get answers. So, whose "fault" is it? To answer this, we must examine the nature of the sickness, the role of anointing oil, and what James means by "the prayer of faith."

Nature of illness:

Was the illness that James refers to physical, spiritual, emotional, or all three? Some cessationists argue that the "weakness" was not physical but spiritual. For example, Ron Blue says, "Many physically ill Christians have called on elders to pray for them and to anoint them with oil, but a sizable percentage of them have remained sick. This fact suggests that the passage may have been mistakenly understood as a physical restoration rather than spiritual restoration."[116] In support of such a view is the seeming emphasis on emotional and spiritual issues and the need for con-

---

114 McReynolds, *Mark*, 57. This incident clearly occurred before the raising of Lazarus. Thus, the disciples would not have had a reason to expect her resurrection. Its chronological relationship to the raising of the widow's son at Nain (Luke 7:11-15) cannot be certain either, though Luke's placing it later gives greater credence to the possibility that the disciples would have already witnessed Jesus' resurrection power.

115 Douglas J. Moo, *The Letter of James*, The Pillar New Testament Commentary (Grand Rapids: William B. Eerdmans; 2000), 234.

116 J. Ronald Blue, "James," in *The Bible Knowledge Commentary: An Exposition of the Scriptures*, ed. J. F. Walvoord and R. B. Zuck, vol. 2 (Wheaton, IL: Victor Books, 1985), 835.

fession of sin. However, most interpreters see James as referring to physical illness. Additionally, the need to call the elders indicates that the person must be "very ill."[117] Similarly, Will Varner rejects the notion of emotional illness and argues for a physical ailment. First, because it is the most common use of the term and, second, because of the implied condition of the person in James. They are "sick enough that the patient cannot go to the πρεσβύτεροι of the church but must have them come to his or her house." He also notes that in this case, "it is the elders who are to be called—not apostles or someone else thought to have the gift of healing."[118] Others note that, though the term can be used for "spiritual weakness," such a meaning is clarified by either a "qualifying" word or the context.[119] Neither is evident in this passage. So, it is better to say that physical illnesses, as a minimum, are in view. Or, if illness in its generic sense is in view, physical illnesses are at least understood to be included.

Anointing with oil:

Those praying for the sick Christian are to "anoint" them with oil. This should lead us to ask, what is the nature of the anointing? Is it medicinal or ritual? Is it connected with the normal medical treatment process or anticipatory to miraculous intervention as representative of the Holy Spirit's anointing? *Aleipsantes*, the term James chooses, is used of perfume as well as oil and has the connotation of common use.[120] The more common term for cere-

---

117 Peter H. Davids, *The Epistle of James: A Commentary on the Greek Text*, New International Greek Testament Commentary (Grand Rapids: William B. Eerdmans, 1982), 192; Kistemaker and Hendriksen, *Exposition of James and the Epistles of John,* New Testament Commentary, vol. 14 (Grand Rapids: Baker Book House, 1953–2001), 175; and Ralph P. Martin, *James*, Word Biblical Commentary (Dallas: Word, Incorporated, 1998), 206, concur.

118 William Varner, *James*, Evangelical Exegetical Commentary, vol. 48 (Bellingham, WA: Lexham Press, 2012), 536-37.

119 Thomas D. Lea, *Hebrews, James*, Holman New Testament Commentary, vol. 10 (Nashville: Broadman & Holman, 1999), 347; Moo, *James*, 237.

120 *Aleipsantes* (ἀλείψαντες) from *aleiphō*. BDAG (William Arndt, Frederick W. Danker, and Walter Bauer, *A Greek-English Lexicon of the New Testament and Other Early Christian Literature* [Chicago: University of Chicago Press, 2000]), 41.

monial anointing is *chriō* (χρίω). It is used in the New Testament figuratively for the Holy Spirit's anointing (Luke 4:18; Acts 4:27; 10:38; 1 John 2:20, and its noun form in 1 John 2:26) and God's anointing of the apostles (2 Cor 1:21) and Christ (Heb 1:9).[121] Trench referred to the former as the "mundane" anointing, with the latter being the "sacred."[122] Noting Richard Trench's distinction, Ron Blue identifies Matthew 6:17 and Luke 7:46 as examples of its use in a non-ceremonial sense. In Matthew 6:17, Jesus commands those fasting to wash their faces and anoint themselves with oil in order to hide their fasting from men. Then, in Luke 7:46, He uses it of a host anointing a guest with oil, a sign of hospitality. Blue concludes, "James is not suggesting a ceremonial or ritual anointing as a means of divine healing; instead, he is referring to the common practice of using oil as a means of bestowing honor, refreshment, and grooming." He says further that the command of Matthew 6:17 for the fasting person to anoint themselves with oil means that James intended to say that "the 'weak' (*asthenei*) and 'weary' (*kamnonta*) would be refreshed, encouraged, and uplifted by the elders who rubbed oil on the despondents' heads and prayed for them."[123]

Based on Jewish and Gentile practices of anointing with oil while praying for the sick person, Peter Davids does not see this anointing being used medicinally but as "either the outward sign of the inward power of prayer or, more likely, a sacramental ve-

---

121 BDAG, 1091. Mary's "anointing Jesus for burial (Matt 26:7; Mark 14:3) is described with *katacheō* (κατέχεεν; to pour out). And Jesus describes it with *myrizō* (μυρίσαι), a term for anointing for burial (BDAG, 661). Thus, neither term is used. In Mark 16:1 the two Marys and Salome come to Jesus' tomb with spices to anoint (*aleipsōsin*; ἀλείψωσιν) Jesus' body. The prostitute's anointing of Jesus' feet (Luke 7:38) is also described with *aleiphō* (ἤλειφεν). Jesus uses the same verb for anointing a guest (ἤλειψας·; Luke 7:46). A related word, (ἐγχρίω), is used in Rev 3:18 when the Church of Laodicea is invited to "smear" or "anoint" their eyes with salve. In John 9:6, John uses *epichriō* (ἐπέχρισεν) to describe Jesus' anointing or smearing clay on the blind man's eyes. The man born blind uses the same verb to describe Jesus' action in verse 11. John 11:2 uses *aleiphō* to identify Mary as the one who anointed of Jesus which is then described in John 12:3 using the same term.

122 Richard C. Trench, *Synonyms of the New Testament*, 9th ed. Reprint (Grand Rapids: William B. Eerdmans, 1950), 136-37.

123 J. Ronald Blue, "James," 834-35.

hicle of divine power."[124] Lenski understands this use of the participle to indicate a body rub in order to soothe the patient is in view.[125] On the other hand, Ralph Martin does not see the text as clear enough to indicate the purpose of the anointing, whether medicinal or spiritual. He correctly notes that enough information on healing practices has yet to be found for us to be sure what is meant. He then warns, "The paucity of data in the NT is itself a caution against drawing too many conclusions regarding early church practice."[126]

However, Mark uses it for the anointing that accompanied the miraculous healings of the apostles (Mark 6:13) when sent to the nation of Israel by Jesus in pairs to announce the nearness of the Kingdom. Since miraculous healings are in view here, James' use of *aleiphō* cannot be restricted to medicinal use. More helpful to interpreting James' instruction is recognizing his use of the anarthrous aorist active participle (*aleipsantes*, ἀλείψαντες), indicating the emphasis is on the command to pray. The anointing with oil is to accompany the prayer but is not the focus of the command.[127]

Prayer in faith:

Faith and presumption, wishful thinking, are two distinctly separate things and need to be differentiated. Faith always has an object that validates it. Faith never operates in a vacuum. As presented in Scripture, faith has God and His promises as its object. When the author of Hebrews says that God's word is "living

---

124 Davids, *James*, 193.
125 R. C. H. Lenski, *The Interpretation of the Epistle to the Hebrews and of the Epistle of James* (Columbus, OH: Lutheran Book Concern, 1938), 661.
126 Martin, *James*, 208. References to the medicinal use or value of oil include the biblical passages of Isa 1:6; Jer 8:22; and Luke 10:34. Extrabiblical sources include Josephus *Antiquities* 17:172; *War* 1:657; Life of Adam and Eve 36; Apocalypse of Moses 9:3; Philo, *Sum.* 2.58; Plato, *Menex* 238; and Pliny, *Natural History* 23.39-40. Though all refer to oil being connected with healing, they do not describe or instruct *how* it was to be administered or the significance of its use beyond soothing pain.
127 Davids, *James*, 193; Kistemaker and Hendriksen, *Exposition of James and the Epistles of John*, 175-76.

and active," he is telling us that God's promises are still in effect (living) and a basis of God's action (active) with respect to His promises and warnings (Heb 4:12).[128] However, that does not apply when someone prays amiss. James alerts us that "amiss" prayers don't get answered (James 4:3).

Sometimes people's prayers are based on a misunderstanding of God's Word, resulting in their requesting something He has not promised. Then, expecting Him to answer, they are disappointed when He does not respond to their request. They "feel" faith and very honestly expect an answer to their prayer. However, to be a valid prayer of faith when claiming a "promise" of God, what they are requesting must be something *God Himself* intended to promise. Faith must be connected to truth. Their prayer is not actually one of faith because they are asking something of God He has not promised or is willing to do. We can still pray in faith (we know God can intervene) even when we do not have a promise. Even so, we cannot have certainty of the answer because we do not specifically know God's will in that particular instance. A proper prayer of faith acknowledges that God *can* act without obligating Him (from our perspective) to act. That faith is one of trust in God, of acknowledging God's ability and right to answer however He chooses. It is not a "name it and claim it" kind of faith, but an "if it is Your will" kind of faith (Mark 1:40-42) that God does respond to when it *is* His will.

There are numerous examples of people who are fully convinced they have been healed and act on the basis of that belief. In that instance, they are experiencing, at least at an emotional level, what they are certain is faith. Yet, their perception of reality, no matter how convinced they are, is wrong because God has not acted. They have not been healed. Keener explains this well.

---

[128] William L. Lane (*Hebrews 1–8*, Word Biblical Commentary, vol. 47A [Dallas: Word, Inc., 1998], 102) uses the term "performative" to summarize the ideas of "living and active." Also, Kistemaker and Hendriksen, *Exposition of Hebrews*, New Testament Commentary, vol. 15 (Grand Rapids: Baker Book House, 1953–2001), 116. Lea (*Hebrews, James*, 71-72) describes it as "dynamic and productive. It causes things to happen."

He describes them as "convinced persons" who "act as though their symptoms do not exist, when in fact no medical change has taken place. While hope and the power of suggestion can exert a positive curative influence in many cases, as doctors also observe, this influence does not prove supernatural intervention. Suggestion can be effective even when the healing practitioner uses deception."[129] Even so, some people do get better. In some of these cases, he notes that they may "stem from emotional or mental cures, whether by strengthening the body's immune responses or by addressing psychological roots of the initial illness. This factor is widely recognized, including by commentators who also allow for organic supernatural cures."[130] His last statement is important to note. While believing that miraculous healings are occurring today, Keener does not suggest that every seeming or claimed healing is miraculous.[131] There can be natural causes for some of them. Thus, as noted earlier, the need for a clear definition of what is a miracle and what is not.

Thomas Lea reminds us that other factors may play into the question of the person's healing. "With these promises God still retains his freedom to do his will and work things out in the ways best for the kingdom. Prayer can bring healing, but lack of healing does not show that the one praying lacks faith. Neither does it show that the prayer is somehow invalid or that God is somehow incapable of healing."[132] Further, he notes that "we cannot take this statement as a guarantee that every prayer offered with a sufficient degree of faith will be answered. The intercessor must approach God in an attitude of faith, but the request will be granted only if it accords with the will of God (1 John 5:14)."[133]

What if that person has a terminal illness that is intended by

---

129 Keener, *Miracles*, 2:610.
130 Ibid., 2:630.
131 Ibid., 2:647.
132 Lea, *Hebrews, James*, 348.
133 Ibid., 348.

God to be terminal? It may be like the difference between Elijah and Elisha. Both were faithful prophets of God who stood for Him against a whole nation in rebellion and faithfully fulfilled their ministries. In many ways, Elisha's ministry was more "kindly" than Elijah's. However, whereas Elijah's ministry ended with him riding a fiery chariot up to heaven, the end of Elisha's story begins with the words, "Elisha had become sick with the illness of which he would die" (2 Kgs 13:14). Numerous examples of this can be found throughout the body of Christ, where individuals are prayed for, but to no avail if deliverance is the only acceptable result of prayer.[134]

The apostle John reminds us in 1 John 5:14-17 that we can have confidence in prayer when we know it is God's will and that sometimes we are to pray concerning the sin we see in another believer's life. We can intercede for them. And, as James (5:15) notes, some illnesses are the result of sin. Others can pray for those sins, and God does forgive them. However, John also alerts us that some sins are serious enough that God will not turn from His decision to terminate the life of the disobedient believer. For those, we should not pray because our prayer will be ineffective. No amount of "faith" will change the result. Why? This goes back to the nature of valid, effectual faith. Faith is only faith—the faith God responds to—if its object is God and accords with His will. Praying for the healing of someone who has "sinned unto death" never accords with God's will, no matter how strongly we believe that God *can* intervene and restore that person's health.

---

134 I remember a local pastor when I was serving in the Army at Fort Eustis, Virginia. He was one of those godly men who was both loved and respected by all, who was having a wonderful ministry that was impacting his flock noticeably. He and his church were having a Thessalonian kind of impact in our area (1 Thess 1:7). At what would seem to be the height of his ministry, he was diagnosed with liver cancer, which in those days was basically incurable and a horrible way to die. Modern medicine has found ways to alleviate some of the sufferings and can sometimes bring about remission. However, back then, it was hopeless, humanly speaking. The Christian community began praying for him in earnest, and some voices expressed concern when God did not intervene. The pastor was heartbroken at their response and issued a plea that, instead of praying for his healing, the Christian community should pray that God would enable him to die well and bring glory to God in that manner. He did die well, and God was glorified. God answered our prayers by giving him grace and strength.

After God struck down Ananias, Sapphira's best friend could have prayed fervently during the three hours that intervened that God would forgive and spare Sapphira. She would have still died at Peter's feet (Acts 5:1-11).

So, what about the prayer for healing that James is talking about? In this case, James seems to imply that this illness is not especially terminal. Using John's language, it is not a "sin unto death." Instead, it is bothersome or debilitating. And so, deliverance is something the sick person can anticipate. But whose faith is determinate in effecting that healing?

Whose Faith?
James uses the example of Elijah's prayer to indicate that God responds to the faith of those who pray. It is not the faith of the person being healed but of those praying for their healing.[135] In James 5, these are identified as the elders of the sick person's church. Thus, it was also to be a group of elders, not an individual.[136] Ralph Martin notes well the change in focus from verse 13, where the individual prays in response to a misfortune (*kakopatheō*, κακοπαθέω), to verse 14 where illness (*astheneō*, ἀσθενέω) creates the need.[137] And it is this prayer, rather than the anointing, that proves efficacious.[138]

So how much faith must the sick person have to be healed? Just enough to call for help. It is the same amount of faith needed for a lost person to be justified when they call on the name of the Lord. This promise was first given through Joel (Joel 2:32) and then repeated by Paul, who introduced it with God's promise in Isaiah 28:16 that whoever believed would not be put to shame

---

135 Davids, *James*, 194.
136 Martin, *James*, 206-207.
137 Ibid., 207.
138 Lenski, *Hebrews and James*, 663; Martin, *James*, 209; Kurt A. Richardson, *James*, The New American Commentary, vol. 36 (Nashville: Broadman & Holman, 1997), 233

or disappointed (Rom 10:11-13).[139] In other words, whoever has enough faith to call on God will never find Him unwilling to respond. So, is it sufficient faith for the sick person to ask others to come to pray for them? After all, that is not a prayer directed to God, is it? Yes, it still counts. It is a call to prayer and an act of obedience and submission to God's appointed leadership within the body of Christ.

Another example of how little faith it takes for God to intervene is seen in the wilderness experience of Israel with the fiery serpents. Jesus refers to this when talking with Nicodemus in John 3:14-15. There Jesus tells Nicodemus, "And as Moses lifted up the serpent in the wilderness, even so must the Son of Man be lifted up, that whoever believes in Him should not perish but have eternal life."[140] Salvation comes with only a look of faith. But why would Jesus choose that incident to illustrate saving faith? First, He would be "lifted up" in the same manner as the bronze serpent. Second, those who "look upon" Him will be saved in the same way that the snake-bitten Israelites looked upon the bronze serpent and were delivered from the fiery serpents' deadly venom. So, how much faith did the Israelites need to be saved? Just enough to look. They could even have been doubting. Many may have looked out of desperation rather than hope, wondering if it could really work. However, regardless of the strength or weakness of their faith, if they looked, they lived. Deliverance from the venom was not dependent on the amount of faith but on the fact of faith. Their faith's effectiveness depended on God's faithfulness to keep His promise, not on their faith's volume, purity, or persistence.

---

139 Paul appears to be quoting from the LXX version of Isa 28:16 which translates the Hebrew (אַל יָחִישׁ "act hastily") with καταισχυνθῇ, which means to disgrace, put to shame, or disappoint (BDAG, 517).

140 *The New King James Version* (Nashville: Thomas Nelson, 1982), John 3:14-15.

So, how much faith must the sick person have? Just enough to ask for help based on God's promise. After asking, he or she has done enough, the responsibility for faith passes to the elders. It is their faith that may fail, not the sick person's. But what if none of the elders have the "gift" of healing?

Neither the gift of healing nor a healer:
James does not command us to call for healers or those with gifts of healing. He commands us to call for elders (James 5:14). Further, nothing in the passage requires or indicates any of the elders would have the gift of healing. We can see this as well in passages such as 1 Timothy 3:1-7 or Titus 1:5-9, where qualifications for elders are listed.[141] The ability to heal is not a requirement. Further, James makes clear that their intervention is to be "anointing" and "prayer," not laying on of hands or rebuking the illness or individually affecting the healing of the sick person. Their ministry is primarily spiritual, as indicated by the reference to the sick person's sins being forgiven. The implication is that the sickness may be caused by sin, though not necessarily.[142] But if sin is present, it will be forgiven. Further, the healing results from the faith of the elders as they pray, not from that of the one seeking healing. It is the corporate prayer in faith of the elders (notice the plural) that is effective. Thus, this healing is an act of God in response to His servants who are responsible for the wellbeing of His flock. Peter Davids says it well when he notes that "this is not the special gift of an individual, unlike 1 Cor. 12:9, 28, 30, but the power of a certain office in the church."[143]

---

141 Davids, *James*, 194; Lenski, *Hebrews and James*, 664.
142 The first-class conditional sentence communicates the idea that the presence of sin is assumed for the sake of argument. The apodosis' future indicative communicates the promise of forgiveness is certain if sin is present.
143 Davids, *James*, 194.

Douglas Moo raises the question of whether the gift of healing may have been less widespread, with the Corinthian church being "an exception" rather than the norm. He notes that healing gifts are not mentioned in Romans 12 or Ephesians 4.[144] This would make better sense of James's instructions. However, it is still an argument from silence, with nothing in James requiring it.

---

144 Moo, *James*, 237-38.

3

Theological Arguments

For The Cessation Of Miraculous Gifts

Various arguments have been posited to explain the cessation of miraculous gifts. The major arguments include patterns from God's past dealings with Israel and Paul's corrective to a divisive issue within the church at Corinth. The first pattern is that of divine intervention through individuals at key junctures in Israel's history, with two generations of miracle workers in each turning point of history. A second argument notes God's silence between the two testaments following the ministry of Malachi until John, Jesus' forerunner, arrived on the scene. A third argument focuses on the meaning of "perfect" in Paul's corrective for the abuse of spiritual gifts by the Corinthian church. The role of spiritual gifts in warning Israel of imminent judgment and authenticating the message of the eyewitnesses of Jesus' ministry has also been argued. Additional lesser points will be examined below.

Pattern of Two Generations of Miracle Workers at Critical Junctions in God's Program

A biblical-theological argument for the cessation of miracles involves the record of Scripture concerning periods of miraculous intervention by God. Each case occurs at significant beginning points in the administration of God's program.[145] The first involved the deliverance of Israel from Egyptian bondage and possession of the promised land—the fulfillment of the land promise in the Abrahamic Covenant (Gen 15) and the birth of the nation of Israel. In this time, God intervened miraculously through Moses and Joshua as He snatched Israel from Egypt and enabled them to drive out the Canaanites from their inheritance. The second involved the beginning of the end of the Northern Kingdom of Israel at the point in time when captivity and exile became unavoidable. God repeatedly intervened through Elijah and then Elisha, judging the wicked while blessing His faithful followers. The third involved the transition from the Old Covenant to the New Covenant programs of God, the beginning of the Church age. God intervened first through Jesus and then the apostles and first-generation saints.

Though God continued to intervene on occasion for His people between Joshua and Elijah and then Elisha and Jesus, He did not provide Israel with miracle workers like Moses, Joshua, Elijah, and Elisha. Though He addressed the nation through prophets and delivered them from enemies, sometimes supernaturally, He did not do so through miracle-working individuals. He still intervened in the history of the nation and miraculously in the lives of individuals, such as Shadrach, Meshach, and Abednego (Dan 3). However, as can be seen, they were recipients of divine intervention, not the agents through whom it came.

---

145 Carl F. H. Henry, *God, Revelation, and Authority*, vol. 6 (Wheaton, IL: Crossway Books, 1999), 392-93.

Moses and Joshua: From Captivity to Kingdom

Moses and Joshua represent the first intervention by God through miracle-working individuals. Though God had revealed Himself to Abraham, Isaac, and Jacob and had revealed prophetic truths through Joseph, it was not until Moses that He empowered an individual to perform multiple miracles. Beginning with Pharaoh and then for the next forty years, Moses was an active miracle worker. Even so, his miraculous deeds came at the command of God and were not exercised at will as such.

Joshua followed Moses as both a leader and a miracle worker. Nonetheless, the number of miracles attributed to him is far fewer than those attributed to Moses. Even so, they were not inferior miracles. The crossing of the Jordan was as powerful an event as Israel's crossing of the Red Sea. However, even more impressive would be the miracle of the sun and moon standing still during the battle of Gibeon (Josh 10:12-14). Thus, though he did not perform as many miracles, Joshua was as much a miracle worker as Moses.

Following the death of Joshua, the judges, though called by God to deliver the nation from its oppressors, were not miracle workers. God did intervene miraculously at times in the lives of the judges. However, He did not give them or subsequent prophets miracle-working authority. For example, though some of his feats were "miraculous," the Spirit-empowered Samson with super-human strength was not performing miracles. Rather, he was the recipient of miraculous interventions by God. Again, rather than Isaiah being a miracle worker, the movement of the shadow was a sign provided by God. Isaiah's role was to deliver the message from God that He was going to bring about the sign, not Isaiah (Isa 38:4-8).

Elijah and Elisha: From Kingdom to Captivity

Elijah and Elisha represent another turning point in God's program with Israel, marked by two generations of miracle workers. Both prophets performed numerous miracles as they dealt with rebellious Israel. That they were miracle workers, performing miracles at will, rather than prophets like Isaiah announcing God's miraculous interventions, can be seen from their conduct. Elijah announced the drought as coming at his command (1 Kgs 17:1). His provision of unending flour and oil for the widow was a miracle performed by him (1 Kgs 17:8-16).[146] The first two groups of fifty soldiers sent by King Ahaziah to arrest Elijah felt the heat of his miracle-working authority (2 Kgs 1:1-12). On the other hand, the raising of the widow's son was not a miracle performed by Elijah but an act of God in answer to Elijah's prayer (1 Kgs 17:17-24).

Elisha continued the miraculous ministry of Elijah following his departure in the whirlwind (2 Kgs 2:11). His first miracle, crossing the Jordan, was clearly conducted at his will as were the subsequent miracles of providing oil to pay a widow's debts, removing poison from the stew, and multiplying bread (2 Kgs 4). On the other hand, as with other prophets, he sometimes served as God's spokesman, and God brought about the miraculous intervention. For example, water for the armies of Israel, Judah, and Edom was provided by God in response to Elisha's intervention (2 Kgs 3). As with Elijah, God answered Elisha's prayer for the Shunammite's son and raised him from the dead (2 Kgs 4:32-37). These miracles served to contrast God's power with the impotency of the Canaanite god, Baal.

Following Elijah and Elisha, God continues to provide prophets. However, they are not miracle-working prophets. God continues to intervene miraculously on occasion, but He does

---

146 Though Elijah announces the miraculous act with, "thus says the Lord," it is still an expression of his will rather than a message communicated from God to the widow through Elijah as His spokesman.

not provide miracle workers during the years following the two miracle workers.

Jesus and the Apostles: From an Old Testament Economy to the Church Age

Jesus and the apostles reflect another two-generation period of miracle workers. Jesus' ministry was characterized by so many miracles that the Gospel writers did not even attempt to recount them all. Then, during His ministry, Jesus transferred His authority to the twelve apostles and sent them to deliver the call to repentance to the nation of Israel (Matt 10; Mark 6:7-13; Luke 9:1-6). Following His ascension, the apostles and other saints were given miracle-working authority. In Acts, Luke recounts both Peter and Paul's use of miracles to heal the sick and raise the dead. He also reports others, such as Philip, who performed miracles among the Samaritans as he passed through their villages and preached Christ (Acts 8:6-7). However, as discussed later, the author of Hebrews speaks of miracles as characteristic of the generation of believers that "heard" Jesus and bore witness to his generation.

The pattern of Jesus and the apostles reflects the transition from God working through the Old Covenant to the New. Their miracles marked the church's birth in much the same way as Moses and Joshua's miracles marked the birth of the nation of Israel. Looking back on Israel's history, the pattern is that miracle workers were not a normative mode of divine intervention in the history of the nation of Israel. God *did* continue to speak through prophets until well after Judah's return from Babylonian captivity. Also, He intervened miraculously at times, such as with Daniel, his friends, and the Babylonian kings. Yet, God did not empower miracle workers throughout most of that history. Thus, we should not expect miracle workers to be a normative part of God's dealings with the church either.

Pattern of the Completion of the Old Testament Cannon

We can see a similar pattern in the writing of Scripture. Beginning with Moses, God inspired various authors to record His revelation in what became our Old Testament. Even so, the writing of Scripture was not a steady process. Rather, at various times Scripture was recorded, and a day came when new revelation ceased. Following Malachi, approximately four hundred years of silence ensued in which Israel had no prophetic voice from God. They were not without revelation, though, for they had their canon of Scripture to guide them. They also had their marching orders from God: "Remember the Law of Moses, My servant, which I commanded him in Horeb for all Israel" (Mal 4:4). Of note is the final word from God. Israel was to wait for the coming of Elijah, who's coming would precede the Day of the Lord, which would be culminated with the coming of Messiah (Zech 12–14; Mal 4:4-6). We know from Gabriel and Jesus that John the Baptist provided the initial fulfillment of that prophecy, announcing Jesus' first coming (Luke 1:17). We also anticipate Elijah's appearance on the planet someday to announce the second coming of Jesus (Matt 11:14; 17:10-12).

The Church was given a similar marching order at the end of Revelation (Rev 22:10-17). We are to be awaiting Jesus' return. We are to be about His business, knowing that we will give an account to Him of our works. Similar to the Old Testament, the written prophetic voice became silent with the completion of the canon.

1 Corinthians 13–14: From Infancy to Maturity

In Paul's letter to the church in Corinth, he addresses the issue of the use and abuse of spiritual gifts. After raising the issue of their abuse, Paul provides the solution, love, and then its practical outworking through church order and an emphasis on the edification of the body, not the individual. In his description of the kind of love that would solve the problem, Paul speaks of "the perfect" that would do away with the partial (1 Cor 13:8-12), which many interpreters see as spiritual gifts.[147]

Interpreters have proposed a range of possibilities for the meaning of "the perfect." These include the completion of the canon,[148] the individual's spiritual maturity, or resurrected life in the eschaton following the return of Christ,[149] to name just three. The challenge to interpretation is Paul's use of a neuter adjective for "the perfect" (τὸ τέλειον) in contrast to "the part" (τὸ ἐκ μέρους). Further, the range of meaning contained within the word easily allows for any of the interpretations. The sense of *teleion* (τέλειον) can include the idea of perfection but is also used to refer to mature adults or someone who is fully developed morally.[150] The verb form of the word can also include the ideas of finishing something, to bring something to its goal, to bring to full measure, or to fulfill prophecy.[151]

The challenge faced is that behind every free-standing adjective is an understood noun or referent. Interpreters continue to pursue the referent of these two neuter adjectives by advancing the following proposed solutions.

Completion of the Canon

A common argument, more prevalent in past years, is the idea that "the perfect" refers to the completed canon of the New Tes-

---

147 Earl D. Radmacher, Ronald Barclay Allen, and H. Wayne House, *Nelson's New Illustrated Bible Commentary* (Nashville: T. Nelson Publishers, 1999), 1 Cor 13:8–10.
148 Kistemaker and Hendriksen, *Exposition of the First Epistle to the Corinthians*, New Testament Commentary, vol. 18 (Grand Rapids: Baker Book House, 1953–2001), 467.
149 David K. Lowery, "1 Corinthians," in *The Bible Knowledge Commentary: An Exposition of the Scriptures*, ed. J. F. Walvoord and R. B. Zuck, vol. 2 (Wheaton, IL: Victor Books, 1985), 536.
150 BDAG, 995.
151 BDAG, 996.

tament.¹⁵² Since *biblion* (βιβλίον) is a neuter noun, Paul's choice of the neuter adjective for "the perfect," would indicate he is referring to Scripture, rather than the person of Christ, which would seem to call for the masculine form of the adjective. The canon would have been completed by the end of the first century with the writing of Revelation. This would coincide roughly with what appears to be the time when miracle workers and the "sign" gifts were disappearing from the scene.

Arguments for this view are as follows. Houghton, identifying prophecy, tongues, and knowledge as "partial gifts," argues, "Both what is complete and what is partial are revelational. So 'the perfect' refers to completed revelation."¹⁵³ Woods argues that Paul's use of the Greek article "the" indicates that "*quantitative completeness* is the best understanding of *teleion*" and so Paul has "the completion of the New Testament canon" in view."¹⁵⁴ This view "defends the continuity between Old Testament prophecy and New Testament prophecy supported by the biblical data" and "maintains the proper link between Paul's statement about these gifts ceasing in 13:8 and his explanation of that statement in 13:9-10" and "gives an interpretation of 'the perfect' in 13:10 that is corroborated by both the grammatical and historical evidence."¹⁵⁵

Arguments against it referring to the canon have arisen among other interpreters and theologians. The first argument is that if this were true, modern interpreters would better understand Scripture and key doctrines than Paul. However, the continued theological debate between godly men and women

---

152 R. Bruce Compton, "1 Corinthians 13:8–13 and the Cessation of Miraculous Gifts," *Detroit Baptist Seminary Journal Volume 9* 9 (2004): 98; William MacDonald, *Believer's Bible Commentary: Old and New Testaments*, ed. Arthur Farstad (Nashville: Thomas Nelson, 1995), 1797.

153 Myron J. Houghton, "A Reexamination of 1 Corinthians 13:8–13," *Bibliotheca Sacra* 153 (1996): 350.

154 Andy M. Woods, "The Meaning of the Perfect in 1 Corinthians 13:8–13," *Chafer Theological Seminary Journal* Vol. 10, 10, no. 2 (2004): 3.

155 Compton, "1 Corinthians 13:8–13 and the Cessation of Miraculous Gifts," 144.

indicates otherwise.[156] Further, the absence of *biblion* from the context makes it unlikely Paul would be referring to Scripture. Usually, pronouns and adjectives that are being used substantively, as here, will have some contextual relationship with a prior reference that clarifies their use. This does not seem to be the case here. Even if it could be demonstrated that the so-called sign gifts had ceased by the time John wrote Revelation, that would not in and of itself strengthen the likelihood that the close of the cannon was in view in this passage. Dwight Hunt points out that "neither Paul nor the Corinthians" were "canon conscience."[157]

"The Church's" or an Individual's Spiritual Maturity

In this view, "perfect" is intended to be understood as "mature." Either the church as the body of Christ or an individual believer has reached the goal of growth intended by God.[158] For example, Timothy Dane writes, "God produced this maturity in the corporate church at some point within the apostolic age, and that the arrival of this maturity is what brought about a cessation to the miraculous gifts. ... it was a maturity that enabled the early church to outgrow the unloving, Jew-Gentile disunity that characterized the early church in the first century."[159] James Scott sees it fulfilled individually.

> In this context, the chief point of vv. 8-12 is that the time will come in the experience of each spiritually gifted Christian when his or her spiritual gifts will come to an

---

156 Pfeiffer and Harrison, *Wycliffe Bible Commentary: New Testament*, 1 Cor 12:9.
157 Dwight L. Hunt, "The First Epistle of Paul the Apostle to the Corinthians," in *The Grace New Testament Commentary*, ed. Robert N. Wilkin (Denton, TX: Grace Evangelical Society, 2010), 752.
158 Knofel Staton, *First Corinthians: Unlocking the Scriptures for You*, Standard Bible Studies (Cincinnati, OH: Standard, 1987), 231.
159 Timothy L. Dane, "Maturity and Cessationism: The Cessation of the Revelatory Gifts with the Arrival of Body Maturity as Foretold by Paul in 1 Corinthians 13:8-13" PhD dissertation, Baptist Bible Seminary, 2016, 19.

end—leaving whatever love (and other fruit of the Spirit) has been cultivated in that person. Paul may incidentally say something about the history of spiritual gifts, but fundamentally he is talking about their cessation in the experience of the persons exercising them. In other words, Paul is not particularly concerned about how long certain gifts will be observable somewhere in the church. Rather, he is concerned about how long they will be functioning in the lives of the Christians who possess them.[160]

Passages such as Colossians 1:28 and James 3:2 are used to support this idea.[161] Paul's use of "the perfect" (τὸ τέλειον) in 1 Corinthians 13:10 and "child" (νήπιος) in verse 11 is repeated in 1 Corinthians 14:20. There Paul, using the same root or word, commanded the Corinthian believers to "be babes" (the imperative: νηπιάζετε) with respect to malice, but to "become mature" (τέλειοι γίνεσθε) —literally "perfect"— in their understanding. He follows this with an explanation of the role of tongues in God's revelatory program serving as a warning to Israel of impending judgment, a judgment fulfilled in AD 66 to 70 with the Roman conquest of Judea and destruction of the temple. It is further argued that the immediate context, Paul's discussion of spiritual gifts, fits better with a focus on spiritual maturity than with an eschatological future. "The purpose of spiritual gifts in the immediate context is the maturity of the church, the edification of believers, and so Paul's use of 'perfect' here should be read in that light."[162] Other representatives of this view include

---

160 James W. Scott, "The Time When Revelatory Gifts Cease (1 Cor 13:8–12)," *Westminster Theological Journal* 72, no. 2 (2010): 27.

161 Doug Redford, *The New Testament Church: Acts-Revelation*, Standard Reference Library: New Testament, vol. 2 (Cincinnati, OH: Standard Pub., 2007), 177; Anthony C. Thiselton, *The First Epistle to the Corinthians: A Commentary on the Greek Text*, New International Greek Testament Commentary (Grand Rapids: William B. Eerdmans, 2000), 1065.

162 Knofel Staton, *First Corinthians*, 231.

Robert Thomas and Dave Farnell of The Master's Seminary.[163]

Understandably, the weakness of this view is that "the maturity of the Church does not come close to the condition Paul is describing in 1 Cor 13:12."[164] Its proponents have difficulty defining what is meant by "maturity." And church history includes periods of regression in maturity, such as during the Dark Ages.[165]

Christ's Return

The majority of interpreters appear to favor the idea of life in the eschaton following Christ's return.[166] Richard Pratt is representative when he says that Paul's "perfection" involves knowledge of Christ that would be gained at His second coming which would involve "meeting Christ in person; therefore, for the church as a whole, it must take place at Christ's second coming—at the consummation of all things in him (Eph. 1:10)."[167] David Garland argues that "the battery of future tenses, the disappearance of the partial replaced by the complete, and the reference to knowing as God knows us, all point to the end time." He sees Paul contrasting the present age with the eschaton, with "the perfect" being "shorthand for the consummation of all things."[168]

---

163 Robert L. Thomas, *Understanding Spiritual Gifts* (Grand Rapids: Kregel, 1999); F. David Farnell, "The New Testament Prophetic Gift: Its Nature and Duration," PhD dissertation, Dallas Theological Seminary, 1990.

164 Hunt, "The First Epistle of Paul the Apostle to the Corinthians," 752-53.

165 Edward B. Dennis, "The Duration of the 'charismata'," (Master's thesis, CBN University, 1989) 75.

166 John D. Barry, et al., *Faithlife Study Bible* (Bellingham, WA: Lexham Press, 2012, 2016), 1 Cor 13:10; C. K. Barrett, *The First Epistle to the Corinthians*, Black's New Testament Commentary (London: Continuum, 1968), 306; Kistemaker and Hendriksen, *First Epistle to the Corinthians*, 467-68; Kenneth Schenck, *1 & 2 Corinthians: A Commentary for Bible Students* (Indianapolis, IN: Wesleyan Publishing House, 2006), 186; Charles H. Talbert, *Reading Corinthians: A Literary and Theological Commentary on 1 & 2 Corinthians*, rev. ed., Reading the New Testament Series (Macon, GA: Smyth & Helwys Publishing, 2002), 109; Ronald Trail, *An Exegetical Summary of 1 Corinthians 10-16*, 2nd ed. (Dallas, TX: SIL International, 2008), 184.

167 Richard L. Pratt Jr., *I & II Corinthians*, Holman New Testament Commentary, vol. 7 (Nashville: Broadman & Holman, 2000), 234.

168 David E. Garland, *1 Corinthians*, Baker Exegetical Commentary on the New Testament (Grand Rapids: Baker Academic, 2003), 622-23.

Dwight Hunt points out that the "Greek word for *perfect* (*teleion*) is never used for the Second Coming. Also, the word is neuter, and Christ is a person. However, the coming of Christ is an event, and even though the word is not used for the coming of Christ, parallel passages such as 1 John 2:28 strongly suggest support for this view."[169] His comments do expose the weakness of this view. Even so, since *teleion* has a wide range of possible meanings and uses, Paul could choose to nuance it with this sense here even though he has not used it with that sense elsewhere. As C. K. Barrett observes, this term is common in Paul's literature (1 Cor 2:6 and 14:20 are examples), and its "precise meaning" is determined by its context. He then notes that here Paul is contrasting *teleion* with *ek merous* (ἐκ μέρους) which is best translated "in part." Thus, the sense of *teleion* is "not perfection (in quality) but *totality*." However, this totality of knowledge cannot be attained apart from the eschaton.[170]

Dane divides this view into four subcategories:[171] The individual eschatology view sees *teleion* referring to completed knowledge that will be experienced by all believers after death or the rapture of the church. When the believer enters Christ's presence in heaven, all knowledge will be complete. Thus, Paul is not addressing the issue of gifts ceasing in this life but of their lack of necessity in the life to come. Richard Gaffin and Thomas Edgar are representatives of this view.[172] The eternal-state view believes that all the spiritual gifts will continue until the end of the millennium when the eternal state comes.[173] John MacArthur is one of the better-known proponents of this view.[174] The non-dispensational and dispensational views have a large num-

---

169 Hunt, "The First Epistle of Paul the Apostle to the Corinthians," 752-53.
170 Barrett, *The First Epistle to the Corinthians*, 306.
171 Dane, "Maturity and Cessationism," 54-92.
172 Richard B. Gaffin, Jr., "A Cessationist View," in *Are Miraculous Gifts for Today? 4 Views*, 55; Thomas R. Edgar, *Miraculous Gifts: Are They for Today?* 340.
173 Dane, "Maturity and Cessationism," 58.
174 John F. MacArthur, Jr., *1 Corinthians* (Chicago: Moody Press, 1984).

ber of adherents who differ in their understanding of the relationship of "the perfect" (τὸ τέλειον) to the *Parousia*. Non-dispensationalists tend to see the gifts continuing up to the coming of Christ, while dispensationalists tend to see them ending before His return.[175]

The Role of Tongues as a Warning of Jerusalem's Destruction

Paul informed the church in Corinth that tongues were given as a sign to Israel, warning of coming judgment (1 Cor 14:20-25). He quotes Isa 28:11-12 and then concludes in the following verses that the purpose of tongues was as a sign to unbelievers. At the same time, prophecy, his preferred gift, was designed to benefit believers. But which unbelievers? It cannot be Gentile unbelievers because of what Paul says about tongues convincing visiting unbelievers that those speaking in tongues are insane (1 Cor 14:23). However, if the tongues Paul refers to here are connected to Isaiah's prophecy, clearly directed at Judah and not Gentiles, they would be warning Judah of coming judgment in Paul's day.

Earlier (1 Cor 12:7-11), Paul had affirmed the common purpose of all spiritual gifts, the common good, and the gift of tongues was included in the list. In his corrections to Corinthian abuses of the gifts, he limited the value of tongues to their ability to edify other believers when interpreted (1 Cor. 14:5-6) and only if the interpretation resulted in communicating revelation, knowledge, prophecy, or teaching. In the context of this discussion, Paul reveals the purpose of uninterpreted tongues as a sign to unbelieving Israel. In light of the Isaiah quotation, it would then motivate unbelieving Israel to ask why the Messianic Kingdom had not arrived and be alerted to their coming judgment.

---

[175] Dane, "Maturity and Cessationism," 56-92.

Further, Paul's words should be seen in the light of Peter's call to his countrymen in Acts 2:40 to "be saved from this perverse generation." It was their generation of Judeans that had crucified Jesus and faced God's judgment. This promised judgment came in the years of AD 66 to 73 during the failed Jewish revolt. God's judgment fell on Jerusalem with its fall to Titus in AD 70 and the subsequent burning and complete destruction of the temple. Even more severely, God's judgment fell again on the nation during the Bar Kokhba revolt in AD 135. It resulted in Jerusalem's complete destruction and the purging of Jews from Judea through the mass enslavement that followed the Roman conquest. This is the same danger the author of Hebrews warned his generation against (Heb 10:25).[176]

With God's judgment completed on Jesus' generation, tongues' role as a sign to Israel would certainly have been completed. As Paul pointed out earlier in the chapter, from that point on, its only usefulness would be if it communicated prophetic truths that edified the church and if there were an interpreter present who could make it edifying by translating the message into Greek. This leads to the question of what role spiritual gifts, in general, played in the early church.

The Authenticating Role of Spiritual Gifts (Hebrews 2:1-4)

Spiritual gifts in the early church served an edifying role within the body of Christ. This is seen in 1 Corinthians 12, where at least a sampling of the spiritual gifts is listed, if not all those given to the church. Today, their present status continues to be debated, with a range of views persisting throughout the Christian community. This ranges from those who believe all are still being manifested regularly today to those who think all or most

---

[176] Allen C. Myers, *The Eerdmans Bible Dictionary* (Grand Rapids: William B. Eerdmans, 1987), 126; Ricky L. Johnson, "Bar-Kochba," ed. Chad Brand, *et al., Holman Illustrated Bible Dictionary* (Nashville: Holman Bible Publishers, 2003), 171.

of the gifts have ceased to be given. As a soft cessationist it seems better to see them as having passed from the scene in the first century, though God can still express them in unique situations that fulfill His purposes. But is there evidence in Scripture that might indicate the passing of the full expression of gifts in the early church?

In the first verses of the second chapter of Hebrews, we learn something about its author and the place of miracles and miraculous gifts in the early days of the church. First, its author is clearly a second-generation Christian. He distinguishes himself from "those who heard" Jesus. This would eliminate him from being one of the apostles or one of the others who followed Jesus during the days of His ministry on earth.[177] A second contribution to our discussion is his linking the spiritual gifts to the first-generation eyewitnesses. He additionally states that these miracles and spiritual gifts functioned to authenticate the message of the eyewitnesses to Jesus' revelation. As discussed elsewhere, he at least implies, if not states plainly (my view), that the gifts and signs were past and no longer happening as the eyewitness generation passed from the scene.

Need for Revelatory Spiritual Gifts Declined with the Growth and Completion of the New Testament Cannon

The Church was born on the day of Pentecost and entered its infancy. The apostles began to write under the inspiration of the Holy Spirit, and new Scripture arose. Their writings would eventually become what we know as the New Testament. During this period of inscripturation, the church moved from infancy to maturity. Its maturity was not the completion of the canon, though the two events may have coincided to some extent. All this tran-

---

177 Even though Paul would fit into this same category and is, in a very real sense, a second-generation apostle, this need not be understood as a possible argument for Pauline authorship of Hebrews.

sition appears to have happened before John's Revelation was penned. We can see this in the writings of the church fathers that preceded John's final contribution to the canon of Scripture.

The apostolic writings, copied and distributed in the first century, contributed to the maturing of the church. Key doctrines were clarified, and issues were addressed. As the churches throughout the known world received and compiled their copies of Scripture and then taught from it, the body of Christ moved toward maturity. Having said this, one must recognize that throughout church history, to this day, there are immature believers within the body of Christ and immature churches as well. However, Christendom has reached a level of knowledge and application vastly different from the first-century churches that awaited their copies of apostolic writings and depended on members with the gifts of prophecy and knowledge to provide them the guidance that Scripture would in later years.

This picture of the church does not assume its maturity could ever be uniform throughout the body of Christ. Some churches are more "mature" than others. However, as a whole, the body of Christ, the Church, can be described as holding to a more-or-less uniform set of key doctrines and practices. Today spiritually mature church leaders are apparent throughout the church worldwide. This is not to say there were no theological debates and heretical teachings persisting at the end of the first century. Theological debate has been a regular occurrence throughout the Church's history. However, in the Church's early years, as the gospel spread throughout the Roman world, especially among the Gentile populations that produced Gentile churches, there would have been churches that could only be described as spiritually immature. We might even point to the church in Corinth as an example of this. Even so, as the century reached its conclusion, the presence of congregations that lacked spiritually mature leadership would have declined to occasional congregations, much as it is today.

Another transition seems to have occurred during the first century. The way God provided spiritual leadership and nurturing changed from gifts to people.

Movement from Spiritual Gifts to Gifted People

If miraculous gifts passed from the church near the end of the first century, then how did God meet the Church's need for instruction and direction? This question can be answered with two points. First, as the universal church distributed the apostles' writings, the canon of Scripture became available. It is through God's revealed word that He chooses to lead. This can be seen with the Old Testament canon. After Malachi was written, there was not just an end to writing prophets. There was also an end to speaking prophets. The "four hundred silent years" between Malachi and John the Baptist came, at least partly, because God did not have anything else to tell them they could not find clearly articulated in the Old Testament Scriptures. More revelation was unnecessary. In the same way, once God was finished speaking to the Church through His apostles and New Testament prophets, the gift of prophecy became redundant. If someone should ask, "God, what is your will?" the answer would be, "Read the text."

In Ephesians, a prison epistle, Paul makes no mention of miracles after having done so many exceptional miracles when he ministered in Ephesus and planted the church (Acts 19:11-12). We might ask, why? The answer seems to be that his failure to mention gifts at all, but rather focusing on the gift of skilled individuals, came because the church needed to focus on faith, hope, and love more than any given gift. It may also indicate, as well, that God's means of meeting the needs of churches had moved from giving supernaturally enabled gifts to individuals to giving individuals to the church, people gifted with teaching, evangelistic, and administrative abilities. Thus, a second reason that the gifts would have passed is that God had provided the church with qualified leaders (elders, deacons, and deaconesses) and skilled individuals who were "gifted" in the non-miraculous sense. We see this in what Paul writes in Ephesians 4:7-16, near the end of his imprisonment and after the transition from an infant church to a mature church. Paul talked about gifts given to individuals within each church body. He now talks about individuals given to the church body to edify it. Where the gifts of 1 Corinthians and Romans met various needs by being distributed among the members, now people are provided the churches. These individuals fulfill the role of "equippers" for ministry. Beginning around the time of Paul's imprisonment until this day, God gives the church individuals the skill and ability to teach others in evangelism, pastoring, and teaching. These are to equip the saints for the work of service, not just do it themselves. Thus, the church's growth and maturity are now the results of instruction, not supernatural provision.

This conclusion, though, should be supported by the evidence of the biblical text even more so than from church history or logical argumentation. So, can it be demonstrated? I believe so. In the following chapter, we shall examine the biblical arguments for the passing of miraculous gifts even as God provided the church with equippers.

4

Biblical Arguments

For The Cessation Of Miraculous Gifts

Acts: Number and Dating of Healings

The record of Acts abounds with miracles, both described and implied. Though few miracle workers are named, Luke's record suggests more were active than simply those whose deeds he recounted. Edgar's understanding of the record of Hebrews 2:3-4 is that it necessarily implies that all the apostles performed signs and wonders.[178] An examination of the evidence of Luke's record has led some men to understand that a decline in miracles occurred during the time period reported by him. Forge's analysis of Acts led him to conclude that "miracles become less prominent in the later chapters of Acts, especially when the gospel turned to the Gentiles and are less evidential than when given

---

178 Edgar, Miraculous Gifts: Are They for Today? 271.

to the Jews."[179] Having made a similar observation, Knuteson concluded: "It wasn't until Acts 13, some twelve years after Pentecost, that the first organized mission venture was made into Gentile territory. However, the vast majority of miracles occur in the first ten chapters. Why? The obvious and scriptural answer is that supernatural signs are for Jews."[180] This view that a decline is noticeable is held by others.[181]

In contrast, Koenig says, "We conclude, then, that the phenomena Paul calls charismata abounded in the early church. They were 'normal' experiences for nearly all the Christians who wrote and first read the New Testament." To effectively critique the view that miracles declined within the time frame of Acts, its record must be placed upon a chronological line, and a decline defended. Also, it might be asked, does not Mark 16:17-18 indicate a continuance of miracles?

The Dating of the Events of Acts

Based on Hoehner's chronology, the events of Acts begin just before Pentecost in May of AD 30.[182] Paul was converted in the summer of AD 35.[183] His first missionary journey began in April of AD 48 and ended in September of AD 49.[184] This was followed by the conflict between Paul and the Judaizers reported in Galatians 2, which then prompted the writing of the letter to the Galatians in the fall of AD 49.[185] The council meeting of Jerusalem recorded in Acts 15 took place in October of AD 49, soon after he had finished his first journey.[186] During his second missionary

---

179 James N. Forge, "The Doctrine of Miracles in the Apostolic Church" (ThM thesis, DTS, 1951), 46.
180 Roy E. Knuteson, "Are You Waiting for a Miracle?" *Kindred Spirit* (Fall 1979), 22.
181 Walvoord, *The Holy Spirit at Work Today*, 41; Forge, "The Doctrine of Miracles in the Apostolic Church," 46.
182 Harold Hoehner, "Chronology of the Apostolic Age" (ThD dissertation, DTS, 1965), 156.
183 Ibid, 204.
184 Ibid, 237.
185 Ibid, 242.
186 Ibid, 244.

journey, which began in May of AD 50 and ended in November of AD 52, Paul wrote to the Thessalonians his two epistles in the summer of AD 51.[187] His third missionary journey, which included a long stay in Ephesus from September of AD 53 until May of AD 56, began in April/May of AD 53 and ended in May of AD 57.[188] After being arrested and imprisoned, Paul began his journey to Rome sometime around August of AD 59.[189] He was shipwrecked on Malta during the winter of AD 59/60 and finally reached Rome in February of AD 60.[190] Paul would have then left Rome as a free man sometime in the spring of AD 62, two years following his arrival.[191]

The Number of Miracles in Acts

Supernatural acts not performed by miracle workers

Certain supernatural events and incidents are not considered miracles by the definition being used for this study. Though they are supernatural, they were not performed through human agency. These include such things as Jesus' ascension (Acts 1:9), visions (Acts 7:56; 9:3-16; 10:3-6, 10-16; 16:9; 18:9), Philip's teleportation by the Spirit (Acts 8:39-40), and angelic activities such as Peter's rescue (Acts 12:7-11) and Herod's demise (Acts 12:20-23). Paul arising after his stoning in which he was left for dead outside Lystra was probably supernatural but not accomplished at the hands of a human agent. Those acts which are considered miracles, since they were wrought through a human agent, follow below.

---

[187] Ibid, 262-66.
[188] Ibid, 295.
[189] Ibid, 311.
[190] Ibid, 319.
[191] Ibid, 321.

APOSTOLIC *Signs and Gifts* OF THE SPIRIT

Single miracles performed by an agent
Within the record of Acts, there are twelve references to miracles having a single beneficiary or victim. These include Peter and John healing the lame man (Acts 3:1-4), Peter pronouncing God's judgment on Ananias and then Sapphira (Acts 5:1-11), Ananias of Damascus healing Saul of his blindness (Acts 9:17), Peter healing Aeneas (Acts 9:32-35), Peter raising Dorcas from the dead (Acts 9:36-42), Agabus prophesying (Acts 11:27-28), Paul blinding Elymas (Acts 13:4-11), healing a lame man (Acts 14:8-10), casting out a demon (Acts 16:16-18), raising Eutychus (Acts 20:7-12), and ignoring the bite of a venomous snake (Acts 28:1-6).

Multiple miracles performed by an agent
There are ten references to multiple miracles in Acts. The multiple miracles are described in terms of signs and wonders, which would include such things as tongues, healings, and raising the dead. For example, the signs of Stephen in Samaria are further described as including casting out demons, healing the paralyzed and lame, as well as "great miracles" (Acts 8:6-7, 13). Thus, in the case of the multiple miracles, healings can be understood as repeatedly and numerously taking place. These ten references include the Pentecost sign of tongues as well as tongues in Cornelius's home (Acts 10:44-48), four references to signs and wonders being performed (Acts 2:43; 5:12; 6:8; 8:6-13; and 14:3), Paul's extraordinary miracles in Ephesus (Acts 19:11-17), and his multiple healings on the island of Malta, beginning with Publius's father (Acts 28:7-9).

The Dating of the Miracles of Acts

Miracles are reported throughout the record of Acts, beginning in the second chapter and ending with Paul healing at will in the last chapter. The miracles can be dated as follows:

DATING THE MIRACLES OF ACTS		
Miracle(s)	Reference	Date
Tongues on Pentecost	2:4	May 27, AD 30
Wonders and signs	2:43	Spring/Summer AD 30
Lame man (Peter & John)	3:1-4	Summer AD 30
Ananias and Sapphira	5:1-11	AD 31-32
Many signs and wonders	5:12	AD 31-33
Wonders and signs	6:8	Early AD 35
Signs in Samaria	8:6-13	May-Summer AD 35
Ananias healed Saul	9:17	Summer AD 37
Peter healed Aeneas	9:32-35	AD 37-40
Peter raised Dorcas	9:36-42	AD 37-40
Cornelius's tongues	10:44-48	AD 40-41
Agabus's prophecy	11:27-28	Spring AD 44
Paul blinded Elymas	13:4-11	April-June AD 48
Signs and wonders	14:3	Oct. AD 48- Feb. AD 49
Paul healed lame man	14:8-10	March-June AD 49
Paul cast out demon	16:16-18	August-October AD 50
Paul gave the Holy Spirit	19:1-7	September AD 53
Extraordinary miracles	19:11-17	Sept. AD 53- May AD 56
Paul raised Eutychus	20:7-12	April AD 57
Paul ignored viper bite	28:1-6	October AD 59
Paul healed all	28:7-9	Oct. AD 59- Feb. AD 60

The time gaps between miracles, whether singular or multiple, do not indicate times of inactivity on the part of the apostles or others. Rather, the miracles performed by them were not included in the record of Acts because they did not help develop Luke's message. The examples given were enough to achieve his purpose for writing.

APOSTOLIC *Signs and Gifts* OF THE SPIRIT

This writer understands that the purpose of Acts was to show the gospel's spread to the Gentiles and that Paul's apostleship was valid.[192] The record of miracles provided by him was adequate to authenticate Paul's apostleship. It also provided historical evidence of the role of miracles in authentication, as described in Hebrews 2:3-4. Thus, instead of a full accounting of all the miracles of the apostolic age, there is provided only a sampling that is adequate for drawing a comparison between the ministries and authority of Peter, the prime apostle, and Paul, the apostle to the Gentiles. As a result, Paul is shown performing the same miracles as Peter. The evidence that these were not the only ones they accomplished is seen in the general statements that they performed many signs and wonders (Acts 2:43; 5:12; 6:8; 14:3; 19:11-17; 28:7-9). Luke recounted some typical examples and reported the unusual ones, such as raising the dead and the ministry of Paul in Ephesus. That he failed to mention miracles in every city and journey does not necessitate or imply that they were not evident throughout Paul's travels. In fact, the reports in Acts 15 given by Paul and his companions en route to Jerusalem imply that their ministry was characterized throughout by the miraculous. This was then turned about and used as authentication of God's choice of the Gentiles for salvation apart from the keeping of the Law.

No Measurable Decline in Acts

Frost and others have argued that a decline in miracle-working activities can be seen within the record of Acts. This has been a necessary element in the argument that miracles declined and ceased in the first century. Frost's observation serves as an ade-

---

192 Acts is the second part of a two-volume work common to the Greco-Roman world. The first volume would cover the life and teachings of the philosopher. The second volume would cover the stories of his followers as they lived out his philosophy. Thus, a part of Luke's purpose in writing Acts was to complete the series for Theophilus and to show the impact of Jesus' teachings on His disciples. Paul was included by Luke as one of Jesus' disciples, as demonstrated by Jesus' call of Paul on the road to Damascus and subsequent appointing him as His apostle to the Gentiles.

quate example of this position. He says, "In reading the record of the Acts, as compared with that of the Gospels, we see a great change in respect to miracles. First, they largely diminish in frequency, and secondly, they alter considerably in kind."[193]

If one places the miracles on a timeline, they occur less often in the latter portion of Acts than in the first few years. Yet this is a deceptive observation. In actuality, the few total reports of miracles, whether singular or multiple, occur at inconsistent intervals within the historical timeline reflected in the record of Acts. Thus, while miracles are described in Paul's first and third journeys, they are not mentioned in his second.[194] This does not necessarily imply that he was impotent for a season, but only that Luke chose not to list any miracles at that point within his narrative. Further, it is noted by Ryrie: "In the third journey Paul is at the zenith of his miraculous powers. At Ephesus, people have only to bring a handkerchief from his person for someone to be healed. Then Eutychus falls out of a window and is taken up alive."[195] Thus, rather than a decline, Paul is seen as remaining effective. His effectiveness is reinforced on Malta by his ability to shake off a viper and heal all who come to him.

The "apparent" decline within the record of Acts is caused more by its emphasis on the apostle Paul, who spent the last six chapters in custody and thus out of circulation, than on the miracle-working ministry of the apostle or the church. He lacked opportunity to perform miracles. He lacked reason. When the opportunity came on Malta, Paul was again seen performing healing miracles at will. Thus, the "decline" cannot be argued based on the sketches of evidence within the record of Acts.

---

[193] Frost, Miraculous Healing, 124.
[194] Paul did cast out a demon in Philippi (Acts 16:18), but I do not see this as a miracle per se. It was an exercise of apostolic authority but involved action in the spiritual realm rather than the natural realm.
[195] Ryrie, "Miracles (or What Happened to Your Handkerchiefs, Paul?)" *Moody Monthly* (September 1980), 82.

Again, it must be pointed out that the reports of miracles within the record provided by Luke were neither the focus of the history nor ever presented as a complete compendium. Rather, they are given as samples of the deeds of the apostles, with some of the more unusual happenings being reported. Nevertheless, Paul's activity on Malta argues for a continuance of his ability to heal at will, at least until that date.

Conclusion

Hillis's examination of the record of Acts led him to conclude that healings were spasmodic rather than continuous during the apostolic time.[196] This is a good analysis based on the evidence given. Still, the general tenor of Acts suggests that there was a fairly regular pattern of miracles accompanying their preaching with the apostles at least. Miracles were the "norm" for the apostles, represented first by Peter and then Paul, at least through the years covered within Acts.

The Epistles: Time of Writing and References to Miraculous Gifts

Placing the epistles on a timeline provides a means of bringing into perspective the epistles' comments and silences concerning miracles. The silence of the latter epistles can only be shown to be significant if they provide an actual contrast between their silence and the other epistles' commentary to the effect that miracles were present. If the record of the later epistles were mixed, with some referring to miracles as a present experience, then the silence of the others would prove meaningless. Still, a united silence would not prove within itself that miracles had ended. Other evidence would need to be provided, such as indications of miracles not being performed at times when they would normally be expected to appear. In this section, the epistles of the

---

196 Hillis, Tongues, Healing, and You! Section 2, 9.

New Testament will be arranged according to their composition order and place on the timeline defended.

When Written

Pre-imprisonment epistles

James. Many commentators agree that the Epistle of James was written early and is probably the first epistle penned. Its author, James the Just, was martyred in the Spring of AD 62, providing the latest date for its composition.[197] Thiessen sees it being written between AD 45 and 48. He points as evidence of an early date to the lack of any reference to the fall of Jerusalem, the death of James in AD 62 or 63, the primitive church order evidenced within the epistle, the readers' presence in synagogues, and his ignoring Gentile issues.[198] Guthrie agrees with Thiessen concerning the evidence but would move its date forward to AD 50, or possibly as late as AD 60, though his preference is toward the former.[199] A period of authorship between AD 40 and the Jerusalem council of Acts 15 is allowed by Davids, based in part on an acceptance of James the Just as its author. Additionally, he understands that the lack of interest in the Jewish-Gentile controversy and the lack of a clearly developed Christology serve as indicators of its early writing.[200] Though arguing against modern miracle workers, Towns sees James being composed late in the apostolic period. He then interprets James' instructions for the sick as indicating an absence of healers at the time.[201] This would be a convenient argument, but the preponderance of evidence indicates an early date of composition. In contrast, Wilkinson uses the same verses to argue, "There is no suggestion in this

---

197 Hoehner, "Chronology of the Apostolic Age," 356-57.
198 Henry C. Thiessen, *Introduction to the New Testament* (Grand Rapids: William B. Eerdmans, 1952), 276-78.
199 Guthrie, "John," 761-64.
200 Davids, *James*, 22.
201 Elmer L. Towns, "Does God Heal Today?" *The Fundamentalist Journal* 2 (June 1983): 37.

passage of James that the healing work of the Church was something abnormal or extraordinary. It was part of the normal routine of Church life.[202]

Galatians. Galatians is Paul's earliest work. Hoehner holds to a South Galatian position and places it in the fall of AD 49 soon after Paul had returned from his first missionary journey.[203] Guthrie agrees, seeing that the South Galatian theory has the fewest problems.[204] Ridderbos places the epistle after the Jerusalem council but still sees its writing occurring around AD 48 or 49.[205] Betz sees AD 50–55 as a likely period for its writing.[206] Those such as Thiessen who hold to a North Galatian theory may place it as late as AD 56. He sees its composition as closer to that of the Corinthian and Roman epistles than the Thessalonians.[207] This would still place its writing before Paul's Roman imprisonment and within the record of Acts when miracles are attested as still occurring.

First and Second Thessalonians. The Thessalonian epistles follow Galatians, written in the summer of AD 51 and connected with Paul's second missionary journey.[208] Hoehner sees the internal evidence of the epistle indicating its writing soon after Paul's visit. For example, he had already preached in Achaia (1 Thess 1:7-8), and Timothy and Silas had just returned from Macedonia (1 Thess 3:6), reporting that the news of their conversions was still spreading throughout Macedonia. Ryrie agrees with Hoehner's location for writing, Corinth, but posits its writing

---

202 John Wilkinson, "Healing in the Epistle of James," *Scottish Journal of Theology* 24 (August 1971): 342.
203 Hoehner, "Chronology of the Apostolic Age," 241-42.
204 Guthrie, "John," 464.
205 Herman N. Ridderbos, *The Epistle of Paul to the Churches of Galatia* (Grand Rapids: William B. Eerdmans, 1953), 31.
206 Hans D. Betz, *Galatians*, Hermeneia—A Critical and Historical Commentary on the Bible (Philadelphia: Fortress Press, 1979), 12.
207 Thiessen, *Introduction*, 216-18.
208 Hoehner, "Chronology of the Apostolic Age," 262-63.

during the previous winter.[209] Thiessen and Guthrie both post an AD 50–51 date for the epistles based on the same arguments.[210] This is still a time of miracle activity, though no direct reference to miracles is made in either epistle. An AD 50–51 date is generally agreed upon and accepted for this study.

First and Second Corinthians. The Corinthian epistles were written during Paul's third missionary journey between AD 56 and 57 based upon Hoehner's chronology.[211] He views 1 Corinthians as written from Ephesus and then 2 Corinthians from Macedonia just before his return to visit them. This is seen to fit the tenor of the letters, especially the expectation of Paul's next visit in 2 Corinthians. Guthrie sees their writings about a year later, and Thiessen pushes them a couple of years earlier.[212] They were written before Paul's Roman imprisonment and reflected a time when he was both mobile and ministering. Writing during his third journey, they reflected on Paul while he was still actively engaged in miracle-working activities. Even so, Wilcock points out that: "At the beginning of 2 Corinthians we find that the Father of mercies and God of all comfort 'comforts us in all our afflictions' (2 Corinthians 1.3 ff). He doesn't deliver us from our afflictions and He doesn't take them away from us, but He comforts us in them, and He does so with the purpose that we may convey the same comfort to other tried souls."[213] His observation shows that in even the apostolic miracle-working days when various miraculous gifts were distributed within the body of Christ that healing was not a guarantee of every believer.

---

209 Ryrie, First and Second Thessalonians, 12-13.
210 Thiessen, *Introduction*, 192-94, 197-98; Guthrie, "John," 566, 579.
211 Hoehner, "Chronology of the Apostolic Age," 292.
212 Guthrie, "John," 441-43; Thiessen, *Introduction*, 203-205, 208-209.
213 Michael Wilcock, "The Apostle Paul and Healing," *Toward the Mark* (May-June 1983), 58.

Romans. Romans followed closely behind the Corinthian epistles. Written from Corinth, Hoehner places its composition during the winter of AD 56–57, agreeing with Thiessen's arguments.[214] Thiessen bases his view on the internal evidence of 2 Corinthians and Romans 15:25-27 concerning the collection for the saints. Where they are anticipated in the letter to the Corinthians, they are now in hand when writing the Roman church. Also, Romans reflects the fact that Paul is about to go to Jerusalem. Gaius and Erastus (Rom. 16:23) are both identified with Corinth.[215] Guthrie and Murray would place it a year or two later, though in the same location regarding Paul's journeys, imprisonment, and other historical incidents.[216]

Prison Epistles

Paul's first Roman imprisonment included the writing of Ephesians, Philippians, Colossians, and Philemon. These would occur between the Fall of AD 60 and the Spring of AD 62 when Paul was released.[217] Abbott argues for Tychicus as the bearer of Ephesians and the references to him and Paul's imprisonment as evidence of their being written around AD 63 and being sent from Rome as a group.[218] Lightfoot agrees with Abbott and connects the epistles further through the similarities in names of people present with Paul and to whom greetings and such are sent. Based on its similarities to Romans, he then argues for Philippians to be early in Paul's imprisonment while the other three occurred late.[219] Thiessen argues for placing Philippians

---

214 Hoehner, "Chronology of the Apostolic Age," 293.
215 Thiessen, Introduction, 226.
216 Guthrie, "John," 396-97; John Murray, The Epistle to the Romans (Grand Rapids: William B. Eerdmans, 1959, 1965, one volume edition published in September 1968), xvi.
217 Hoehner, "Chronology of the Apostolic Age," 327-28.
218 T. K. Abbott, A Critical and Exegetical Commentary on the Epistles to the Ephesians and to the Colossians, The International Critical Commentary (Edinburgh: T. & T. Clark, n.d.), xxix-xxx.
219 J. B. Lightfoot, St. Paul's Epistle to the Philippians (London: Macmillan & Company, 1913; reprint ed., Grand Rapids: Zondervan, 1953), 31-46.

later than the other three based on Paul's expectation of release and the gospel's spread through Rome.[220] Hoehner, reflecting on Paul's imprisonment as a key to dating the prison epistles, and seeing Ephesians as silent concerning his release, places Philippians after the other three in the spring of AD 62.[221]

This study places Philippians after the other epistles and sees it being written just before Paul's release. This is of special importance since the illness of Epaphroditus is detailed in this epistle and serves as the first indication of a loss of miracle-working or healing ability by Paul. The previous epistles give no evidence of any failures to heal on the part of Paul, and his healing activity on Malta (Acts 28:1-10) indicates he still had miraculous authority as he approached Rome just two years previously.

Pastoral Epistles

First Timothy. Paul's first letter to Timothy was written following his first Roman imprisonment and before his second. First Timothy could have been written anywhere between the late Spring or early Summer of AD 62 to sometime in AD 66, just before Paul's recapture. Thiessen sees 1 Timothy being written three years following Paul's release from his first Roman imprisonment. This allows for a year of ministry in the Asian region and two years in Spain. This assumes a Spanish ministry and allows time for heresies and opposition to develop in Ephesus which are seen as the causes of the letter to Timothy, who had been left in charge of the church by Paul.[222] Guthrie, recognizing the possibility, but not provability, of a second Roman imprisonment preceded by travels, places this epistle in close proximity to Titus and sees them both being written soon after Paul's release from Rome.[223]

---

220 Thiessen, Introduction, 250-51.
221 Hoehner, "Chronology of the Apostolic Age," 325-28.
222 Thiessen, *Introduction*, 262-63.
223 Guthrie, "John," 623.

Though the time is uncertain, its place relative to the other epistles is generally accepted, after the imprisonment epistles and before Titus and 2 Timothy.

Titus. The similarity in content and style with 1 Timothy has led Thiessen to place this epistle close to it rather than near the end of Paul's ministry, as is his second epistle to Timothy.[224] Hoehner, on the other hand, disagrees and sees Paul as first completing his travels to Asia Minor and Spain, then leaving Titus in Crete on his way back to Asia Minor, and then writing him soon after Titus had begun his ministry on the island.[225] The decision on dating hinges a great deal on the possible travels of Paul following his Roman imprisonment. Nevertheless, all agree on the relative placement of the epistle within the framework of Paul's life, namely, that it was written between the two epistles to Timothy.

First and Second Peter. The first epistle of Peter was also written during the general time period of Paul's activities between Roman imprisonments, with the second epistle coming near the end of both Peter and Paul's ministries. The first epistle is seen by Thiessen as reflecting an awareness of Paul's earlier writings and his prison epistles, thus indicating a date after Paul's first imprisonment. The lack of mention of martyrdoms and imprisonments may also argue for a date before Nero's persecutions had begun in earnest. Thus, he sees a date around AD 65 as reasonable for the first epistle. Second Peter is believed to follow soon after his first epistle and to precede his death by only a short time.[226] Guthrie understands the persecutions to be more serious and links the first epistle to Nero's reign. Even so, based on Peter's attitude of submission to the governing authorities, he places it before AD 64 when Nero began persecution in earnest.[227]

---

224 Thiessen, *Introduction*, 266.
225 Hoehner, "Chronology of the Apostolic Age," 347.
226 Thiessen, *Introduction*, 284-85, 290-91.
227 Guthrie, "John," 795-96.

For the purposes of this study, the location of the epistles during the time period following Paul's first imprisonment is accepted. The reference to Paul's writings in 2 Peter 3:15-16 indicates the letters came from Peter nearer the end of his ministry and Paul's.

Second Timothy. Second Timothy reflects Paul's last thoughts as he anticipates execution. The epistle reflects his harsher treatment and expectation of execution in contrast to his enthusiasm and expectation of release found earlier in Philippians. Hoehner sees it being written during the fall of AD 67 after he had been reimprisoned, with Paul's execution coming in early AD 68.[228] This is agreed upon on the part of both Guthrie and Thiessen.[229]

Hebrews. The letter to the Hebrews is the last of the epistles written before the fall of Jerusalem in AD 70. Its date can fall anywhere between AD 67 and 69. If someone besides Paul is seen as its author, its dating can be as late as AD 69 without problems. If one holds to a Pauline authorship, the epistle must be placed during his second imprisonment since there is no indication of Timothy being imprisoned with him the first time. Thiessen sees it as probably being written soon after Paul's death because Timothy is referred to in Hebrews 13:23 as recently being released. Since Paul requested that he come to him in Rome in his last epistle to Timothy, it can be surmised that he was temporarily imprisoned with Paul when he brought him his cloak and parchments (2 Tim 4:13). Secondly, the references to the temple in Jerusalem are in the present tense and reflect its existence and continuing ministry. This leads Thiessen to place the epistle between Paul's execution and the destruction of Jerusalem. Thus, a date between AD 67 and 69 is acceptable.[230] Guthrie does not

---

228 Hoehner, "Chronology of the Apostolic Age," 348-52.
229 Guthrie, "John," 623; Thiessen, *Introduction*, 269.
230 Ibid, 303-304.

consider the present tense verbs to be a weighty argument but does see the lack of mention of the temple's destruction as significant. Still, he sees two dates as probable, that being just before either Nero's persecution or the fall of Jerusalem, depending on the original recipients.[231] Nolland, recognizing that an early date could be argued based on the statement in Hebrews 12:4 that the readers had not resisted to the point of shedding their blood, still opts for a date between AD 66 and 70. He looks to the author's failure to mention the destruction of the temple and says further, "Some passages in the epistle gain in force if we think of a time not long before" (AD 70) "when there was a compelling call to loyal Jews to cast in their lot with those fighting against Rome."[232] The reference to Timothy's release from prison, which, when understood in light of Paul's request for his coming to him in 2 Timothy, provides evidence that the epistle was written after Paul's second imprisonment. The lack of mention of the temple's destruction, in turn, points to a date before the fall of Jerusalem. This places the epistle late, with only Jude and John's writings potentially later.

Jude and John's epistles. Jude and the epistles of John occur following the fall of Jerusalem.[233] They have no mention of miracles as a present experience for the church and so are not being referred to in this study, though Miller sees their silence as significant to the argument for an end to miracles. He states, "It is most interesting to note further that four books (John's epistles and Revelation) were written after the destruction of Jerusalem, and in them not the slightest reference is made to the presence of these spiritual gifts."[234] If a decline can be measured, it should have been evident by the fall of Jerusalem. Their silence is not

---

231 Guthrie, "John," 716-18.
232 Leon Morris, "Hebrews," in *The Expositor's Bible Commentary*, vol. 12 (Grand Rapids: Zondervan, 1981), 8.
233 Guthrie, "John," 883-84, 894, 898; Thiessen, *Introduction*, 295-96, 321-23.
234 Wayman D. Miller, *Modern Divine Healing* (Fort Worth: Miller Publishing Co., 1956), 317.

seen in this study as necessary evidence for a decline, though it is noted that they are all silent concerning miracles in all except the warning passage of Jude and the eschatological portions of the Revelation.

Koenig sees 1 John 4:1ff as alluding to "the charismatic phenomena of prophecy and miracles as events in the church's life."[235] Yet the instruction of John need not necessarily be understood in that light. Bruce points to the instructions of 1 John 4:2 as the key to discernment, referring back to the Old Testament test of prophets in Deuteronomy 13:1-5 and 18:22, along with Paul's warnings in 1 Corinthians 12:3.[236] Marshal agrees.[237] Of note is John's failure to enjoin his readers to exercise the gift of discernment of spirits. Rather, their discernment was to be on a purely natural basis, namely, knowing doctrine and seeking a clear and proper confession. Thus, 1 John 4:1ff is not an allusion or statement indicating miraculous gifts were still in effect.

Conclusion: Time of Writing

Though the date of any given epistle could be questioned, their relative positions regarding historical events and each other are more clearly agreed upon. The writing of James, Galatians, the Thessalonian and Corinthian epistles, and Romans occurred before Paul's first Roman imprisonment and when apostolic miracle-working was present and expected. During his imprisonment, Paul sent letters to the Ephesians, Colossians, Philemon, and then to the Philippians just before his release. After this came the writing of his first epistle to Timothy and a letter to Titus. During the same time period, Peter penned at least his first epistle. With a second imprisonment in Rome came Paul's

---

[235] John Koenig, *Charismata: God's Gifts for God's People* (Philadelphia: The Westminster Press, 1978), 96.

[236] F. F. Bruce, *The Epistles of John* (Grand Rapids: William B. Eerdmans, 1970), 103-105.

[237] I. Howard Marshal, *The Epistles of John*, NICNT (Grand Rapids: William B. Eerdmans, 1978), 203-10.

final letter, addressed again to Timothy and reflecting his imminent death. Similarly, Peter wrote his final letter near the time of Paul's since he died under the same persecution as Paul. Finally, Hebrews was written following the death of Paul and before the destruction of Jerusalem in AD 70.

References to Miracles in the Epistles

Looking to the epistles for answers has been problematic. As Graham Twelftree well notes, "Notably, there is a paucity of immediately obvious data from which we can answer our questions. Not only is our Pauline corpus incomplete, but what we have that most likely comes from Paul's hand, on first reading, has little to say about him in relation to the miraculous, and perhaps nothing to say about him performing miracles."[238] I would differ from him with respect to the completeness of the Pauline corpus but agree that Paul does not say a lot. However, when viewed chronologically, his epistles do hint at a decline.

Their relation to the timeline

Paul's Roman imprisonment appears to be the demarcation point between the period of miracles and the beginning of the church's present experience. Every epistle written before Paul's imprisonment either refers directly or alludes to miracles as a present experience of the church. These include James, Galatians, both Thessalonians, both Corinthians, and Romans. These epistles assume the experience on the part of their readers. The record of Acts indicates a continuance of miracle-working by apostles and others during this period as well. Then, with Paul's imprisonment comes a silence in the prison epistles and all other writings following them concerning any present experience of miracles.

---

238 Twelftree, Paul and the Miraculous, 17.

Only in Hebrews, which was written between Paul's death and the fall of Jerusalem, is there a direct mention of miracles, and then in the past tense.

Epistles viewing miracles as a present experience
Direct references. In his letter to the Galatians, Paul pointed to the miracles occurring among them as proof of God's work in their midst, apart from the Law. He says, "Does He then who provides you with the Spirit and works miracles among you, do it by the works of the Law, or by hearing with faith?" (Gal. 3:5) "Provides" and "works" are present participles describing God. Their action is linked to the verb, which is understood rather than present in this verse.[239] In this rhetorical question, the description of God is one of presently doing those things in the experience of the recipients of the letter. This would fit well with the testimony of Acts since Luke records many miracles occurring during the time of Paul's first missionary journey (Acts 13:4-11; 14:3, 8-10). That miracles were accomplished in the Galatian churches is also testified to by Paul and Barnabas's report to the Jerusalem Council in Acts 15:12. Based on the record of Acts, miracles would be expected and considered the normal experience of the Galatian churches. Thus, Paul's reference is both in line and expected. Its place in the argument of his letter fits, with the emphasis not on the miracles themselves but on their value as evidence of God's work in their midst.

In Paul's letters to the Corinthians, the presence of miracles in the experience of the church is still evident. Chapters 12 through 14 of the first epistle present spiritual gifts and miracles as both operative and normal. In his second letter, Paul points to his own miracles as evidence of his apostleship when he writes, "The signs of a true apostle were performed among you with all perseverance, by signs and wonders and miracles" (2 Cor 12:12).

---

239 A. T. Robertson, *A Grammar of the Greek New Testament* (Nashville: Broadman Press, 1934), 891.

That he is still able to perform miracles at the time of writing this epistle is clear in his less than veiled threat to his opponents when he says, "For this reason I am writing these things while absent, in order that when present I may not use severity, in accordance with the authority which the Lord gave me" (2 Cor 13:10). Hughes understands his words to mean "he has indeed made it perfectly plain that this time he will come and exhibit his authority by inflicting stern punishment on any who deserve it."[240] These epistles occur during his third missionary journey, in which Luke reports miraculous activities, including the extraordinary miracles in Ephesus. Thus, we see that Paul not only sees the Corinthian believers as capable of working miracles, such as healing, but performed miracles at the time he writes to them. Paul's claim in 2 Corinthians 12:12 that he performed the "signs of a true apostle" does not mean that the Corinthians did not see any miracles in their midst apart from his presence. Rather, the signs and wonders performed by Paul are significantly superior to spiritual gifts.

Lastly, Romans reflects miracles as a present experience. In the last of his letter to the church in Rome, he refers to his apostolic authority by saying, "For I will not presume to speak of anything except what Christ has accomplished through me, resulting in the obedience of the Gentiles by word and deed, in the power of signs and wonders, in the power of the Spirit" (Rom. 15:18-19). Paul points to his demonstrated power at this time as proof of apostleship. Though he is looking at past deeds in this passage, there is no inference that miracles have ceased or that they should expect that Paul would be unable to demonstrate his authority similarly should he come to see them.

---

[240] Philip E. Hughes, *The Second Epistle to the Corinthians*, NICNT (Grand Rapids: William B. Eerdmans, 1962), 485.

Indirect reference

The possible references to miracles in Paul's letters to the Thessalonians are less clear than in his letter to the Galatians. In 1 Thessalonian 1:5, he writes, "For our gospel did not come to you in word only, but also in power and in the Holy Spirit and with full conviction." Here the reference to power might refer to the exercise of apostolic authority while in their midst, though the absence of descriptive terminology such as "signs and wonders" in 2 Corinthians 12:12 indicates otherwise.[241] Frame argued against miracle-working power in favor of its meaning of spiritual power.[242] Likewise, Bruce understands the use to refer more to spiritual power and to be related to conviction more than works.[243] Neil says, "With power (*dynamis*) here does not mean, as it sometimes does in the epistles (usually in the plural), outward signs of the presence of the Holy Spirit during a campaign, such as speaking with tongues, healing, and other miracles, but simply the sense the preachers had themselves that their message was striking home."[244]

The strength of this position is the relationship of power to conviction. It is interesting to note that Acts does not mention any miracles being worked while Paul was in Thessalonica, but this silence is not evidence of a lack of activity. It is simply not necessary for such a comment to be made since Luke is reporting miracles during both the first and second missionary journeys. In 2 Thessalonians 2:9, Paul prophecies that the antichrist will come "with all power and signs and false wonders." This indicates future miraculous activities in a negative sense but says nothing concerning miracles as a present experience, other than

---

[241] I. Howard Marshall, *1 and 2 Thessalonians*, NCBC (Grand Rapids: William B. Eerdmans, 1983), 53-54.

[242] James E. Frame, *Epistles of St. Paul to the Thessalonians*, ICC (Edinburgh: T. & T. Clark, 1912), 269.

[243] F. F. Bruce, *1 and 2 Thessalonians*, Word Bible Commentary (Waco: Word Books, 1982), 15.

[244] William Neil, *The Epistle of Paul to the Thessalonians*, The Moffatt New Testament Commentary (New York: Harper, 1950), 17.

that miracle-working per se was not to be viewed as sure proof of one being sent from God. Further, it indicates false miracles since the term for "false" describes all three; power, signs, and wonders.[245] It would then presuppose the readers were acquainted with legitimate signs and wonders.

Epistles' silence concerning miracles
All of Paul's epistles written either during his first Roman imprisonment or after are silent concerning miracles as a present experience of the church.[246] These include Ephesians, Philippians, Colossians, and Philemon, written during his first Roman imprisonment, both epistles to Timothy and his letter to Titus. Further, they make no comment whatever concerning miracles, including healing. In addition, where Paul had connected his apostleship with miracles when writing to the Romans and Corinthians, he was silent concerning them before Timothy (1 Tim 2:7).

One epistle views miracles as a past experience
The letter to the Hebrews is the only epistle that refers to miracles as a past experience. Its only reference to miracles occurs within the context of its teaching of the superiority of Christ over angles and the importance of His gospel. It connects miracles to the apostles and those who heard Jesus' teachings. The author identifies himself as part of the second generation.[247] Thus he would have received his instruction from eyewitnesses but was not one of them.[248] The inference made from this link is that

---

245 Frame, *Thessalonians*, 269. The descriptive genitive *pseudous* (ψεύδους) relates to all three dative feminine and neuter nouns.

246 Forge, "The Doctrine of Miracles in the Apostolic Church," 53.

247 Kistemaker and Hendriksen, *Hebrews*, 59; Lane, *Hebrews 1–8*, 39; Robert J. Utley, *The Superiority of the New Covenant: Hebrews*, vol. 10, Study Guide Commentary Series (Marshall, TX: Bible Lessons International, 1999), 23.

248 Lea, *Hebrews, James*, 24. Westcott (B. F. Westcott, ed., *The Epistle to the Hebrews the Greek Text with Notes and Essays*, 3rd ed., Classic Commentaries on the Greek New Testament [London: Macmillan, 1903], 39) notes that the author's use of the preposition *eis* "suggests an interval between the first preaching and the writer's reception of the message."

with the passing of the generation that heard Jesus, the passing of miracles would necessarily come since the miracles are linked explicitly to eyewitnesses. This is made clear by the author's use of a present participle, *sunepimarturountos*, to describe God's endorsement of the testimony of the witnesses.[249] As David Allen notes, this use of the participle in this construction "means that God joins the witness of the early preachers to confirm the truth of their witness by performing attendant miracles concomitant with their preaching of the gospel."[250] Edgar sees tongues and healings along with other miracles as the signs and wonders spoken of in Hebrews 2:3-4. He says:

> The subject discussed is the salvation which was confirmed to the addressees of the Epistle by those who actually heard the Lord. They were eyewitnesses of the Lord and were therefore the first generation of Christians. God bore witness together with them . . . by the miraculous signs. This was a thing of the past by the time the Epistle was written. The verb "was confirmed" . . . is past (aorist) tense. Apparently this confirmation was not going on at the time of writing. The present tense of the participle, "bearing witness," relates to the main verb, "was confirmed." God was not bearing witness at the time Hebrews was written, but He bore witness by the miracles at the past time, when the eyewitnesses testified to the Hebrews.[251]

Paul Ellingworth and Eugene Nida recognize the direct inference of the first generation but feel that the phrase is vague enough to include the testimony of second-generation Christians who had heard it from first-generation Christians. How-

---

249 BDAG, 969. It means literally, "to testify at the same time."
250 David L. Allen, *Hebrews*, The New American Commentary (Nashville: B & H Publishing Group, 2010), 196.
251 Edgar, Miraculous Gifts: Are They for Today?, 269.

ever, this makes the distinction between eyewitnesses and the author's generation meaningless, and thus the sentence would be redundant.[252] Kistemaker sees the miracles passed, but spiritual gifts continuing till today. Grammatically, though, both are linked together in the thought of the sentence.[253]

Seeing miracles as serving the purpose of authentication, Sywulka says, "The messengers whose witness was miraculously confirmed are described as 'them that heard' . . . , that is, that heard the salvation message spoken by Christ."[254] Understanding the signs as being given by God primarily for the Jews, he sees those signs as "a specific confirmation, related to the spoken proclamation of a revelation, the original hearers of that revelation, and a particular nation to whom the proclamation was made."[255] Thus for him, the signs were principally given for the sake of the Jewish nation. Ryrie understands the statement as indicating that Christ's promise that others would do the same works He did is reported as having been fulfilled by this passage.[256] He says further:

> There were foundational gifts of apostles and prophets (Eph. 2:20), which gifts do not appear in the periods of building the superstructure of the church. Those who were contemporary with Christ experienced certain miraculous gifts of the Spirit which were not experienced by the generation which followed Him (Heb. 2:3-4).[257]

This epistle, then, links miracles to authentication of the message and messengers and does not intimate that they were to be something continued. In contrast, it indicates that mira-

---

252 Paul Ellingworth and Eugene Albert Nida, *A Handbook on the Letter to the Hebrews*, UBS Handbook Series (New York: United Bible Societies, 1994), 30.
253 Kistemaker and Hendriksen, *Hebrews*, 61.
254 Sywulka, "Contribution of Hebrews 2:3-4," 43.
255 Ibid, 47.
256 Ryrie, "Miracles (or What Happened to Your Handkerchief, Paul?)," 83.
257 Ryrie, The Holy Spirit, 84.

cles were something once experienced by the church, something of which the readers were personally aware, but also something they would not expect to be continuing since the miracles served as an effective warning to all generations to follow concerning the danger of neglecting "so great a salvation" (Heb. 2:3).

Conclusion

The record of the epistles, when placed within the timeframe of Paul's travels and the spread of the church, reflects a pattern concerning miracles. Those written before Paul's Roman imprisonment reflect a church in which miracle workers were present, and miracles were a normal experience. By normal, it is meant that God was still actively authenticating the gospel message in that generation through "signs and wonders and by various miracles and by gifts of the Holy Spirit according to His own will" (Heb 2:4). With the imprisonment of Paul comes a silence concerning miracles in all epistles (including Peter, Jude, and John's). This silence is only broken by the reference to miracles in the past tense in the letter to the Hebrews. Though this does not in itself prove their cessation irrefutably, it does imply it. Even so, such a conclusion must be supported by further evidence and reasoning to be significant in the argument for a decline of miracles within the time period of the apostles and the New Testament church.

5

Historical Arguments

For The Cessation Of Miraculous Gifts

Biblical History: The Men Paul Did Not Heal

Within the corpus of Paul's epistles, we come across an endorsement, medical advice, and a passing notation related to three men who were close associates of Paul. They were valued members of his apostolic team. They were needed. Yet in each instance we find them either left by Paul in their state of illness or sent by Paul to someone to assure them of their recovered health. These do not fit comfortably within a picture of Paul with limitless spiritual power to heal. This is the same Paul whose sweatbands healed people miles away while planting the church at Ephesus. This chapter will examine these three men and what Paul says to or about them. This will then provide the background from which we may address the question of Paul's not healing them.

APOSTOLIC *Signs and Gifts* OF THE SPIRIT

Epaphroditus

Epaphroditus' place in the life of Paul is that of a messenger sent to provide him both sustenance and assistance. His name indicates that he was probably a convert out of a pagan family which had named him in honor of the goddess Epaphrodites.[258] His appearance in the letter to the church in Philippi is the only record of him in the New Testament. Though Epaphras may be a shortened form of his name, it is impossible to link him to the Epaphras of the epistle to the Colossians (Col 1:7; 4:12) or even the one named as Paul's fellow-prisoner in his letter to Philemon (Phlm 23). In fulfilling his purpose, Epaphroditus reflected the love and loyalty of the Philippian church to Paul.[259] Lightfoot describes him in this way: "Their zealous attention was worthily seconded by the messenger whom they had chosen. Not content with placing this token of their love in St Paul's hands, Epaphroditus devoted himself, heart and soul, to the ministry under the Apostle's guidance."[260] He was the ideal assistant who gave himself completely to Paul's service.

His place in the timeline

Epaphroditus ministered to Paul sometime between the middle and close of Paul's first Roman imprisonment. This is seen in Paul's expectation of release in his letter to the Philippians (Phil. 2:24). As noted earlier, the Philippian epistle is placed very near Paul's release. So Epaphroditus' arrival must also be somewhere in the latter half of Paul's imprisonment, with his arrival occurring before Paul received word of release. His illness could have occurred during the time period in which Paul was going through being released from Roman house arrest after his case

---

258 F. W. Beare, *A Commentary on the Epistle to the Philippians*, 2nd ed. (London: Adam & Charles Black, 1969), 97-98; Fred B. Craddock, "Philippians" in *Interpretation* (Atlanta: John Knox Press, 1985), 51.

259 J. A. Motyer, *The Message of Philippians: Jesus our Joy* (Downers Grove: InterVarsity Press, 1984), 143.

260 Lightfoot, *Philippians*, 61.

had been dismissed or concluded.²⁶¹ Hoehner sees the length of time for processing a release following acquittal to have possibly lasted as much as six months.²⁶² Thus, assuming Epaphroditus was sent while Paul was still awaiting trial, he would have arrived closer to the middle of Paul's imprisonment than to its end. This would then allow sufficient time for his illness to run its course, for news and messages to travel between Rome and Philippi, and Paul to still be awaiting the final outcome of his trial when he wrote to the Philippians.

The circumstances and nature of his illness
Epaphroditus likely fell ill soon after his arrival in Rome. Nothing is provided within the text of Scripture to reveal the exact timing of his physical decline or what specific illness beset him, but only that it was life-threatening. He may have overextended himself in his desire to serve Paul, which either triggered the illness or exacerbated its intensity. Whether his illness began during the trip to Rome or soon after arriving, it had to be of sufficient length and severity to allow time for the Philippian church both to learn of it, to warrant their concern, and for their concern, in turn, to be communicated back to Rome. Beare argues for enough time between Epaphroditus' arrival and the writing of Philippians for news of his illness to reach home and word to return to Rome, which was more than eight hundred miles apart.²⁶³ Lenski observes, "Surely, as was the custom especially when funds were sent, the Philippians had not sent Epaphroditus alone but had sent others to Rome with him. These had to return alone when Epaphroditus became sick. Paul most certainly sent his thanks for the gift with these messengers and thus knew that the Philippians were informed in regard to Ep-

---

261 W. M. Ramsay, *The Teaching of Paul in Terms of the Present Day* (London: Hodder and Stoughton, 1913), 365.
262 Hoehner, "Chronology of the Apostolic Age," 320.
263 Beare, *Philippians*, 98.

aphroditus even as the latter knew that they were anxious about him."[264] Thus he understands that the group from Philippi likely remained with Paul for several days before returning home. This would also explain how the church in Philippi could hear of his illness and become concerned. The others who accompanied Epaphroditus to Rome returned home with the news that he was critically ill and in danger of death.

Paul's deep concern for him and consternation at the severity of his condition is reflected in the phrase, "God had mercy on him, and not only on him but also on me lest I should have sorrow upon sorrow" (Phil 2:27). Along with the phrase "he came close to death" (Phil 2:30), this indicates that the illness was potentially fatal, possibly even having a normal expectation of death. It has been suggested that his condition may have resulted from an acute infection, but this can only be speculation.[265]

The evidence does point toward his illness being related to physical exhaustion. Motyer understands his condition to have resulted from "a calculated risk which involved the expenditure of all he had."[266] Based on the implied meaning of *paraboleusamenos* (lit. "having gambled with his life"), Lightfoot also argues for Epaphroditus' illness resulting from something like exhaustion or what would normally be considered unnecessary exposure.[267] Bruce agrees with him and says, "Epaphroditus of Philippi overtaxed his strength and suffered an almost fatal illness in his anxiety to be of service to the imprisoned apostle."[268] Martin argues for something more than an accidental illness since risking his life "suggests some deliberate action on his part, not the ill-wisdom of setting out at the wrong season of the year for travelers."

---

264 R. C. H. Lenski, The Interpretation of St. Paul's Epistles to the Galatians, to the Ephesians, and to the Philippians (Minneapolis: Augsburg Publishing House, 1961), 694-95.
265 John Wilkinson, *Health and Healing* (The Handel Press, 1980), 110.
266 Motyer, *Philippians*, 144.
267 Lightfoot, *Philippians*, 124-25.
268 Bruce, 1 and 2 Thessalonians, 457.

However, he relates the illness to a nervous disorder that was aggravated by worrying about problems back in the church at Philippi.[269] Beare understands the "risking his life" to refer to another danger he was exposed to other than illness.[270] The passage's context and the reference to his being sick in verses 26 and 27 make Beare's position unacceptable. Whether exhaustion or exposure, the risk to his life was evident by Paul's expressed concern, "lest I should have sorrow upon sorrow" (Phil. 2:27). The illness threatened to do more than just incapacitate him for a season.

Paul's need to heal

Epaphroditus was sent by the Philippians to minister to Paul while he was still in prison. Paul's letter reveals his view of Epaphroditus, referring to him as his "brother, fellow worker and fellow soldier" who served as their "messenger and minister" to his needs (Phil 2:25). Lenski sees Epaphroditus' role as more than that of a courier, but as someone sent to assist Paul, both to serve him and serve with him, in the furtherance of the gospel while he was incarcerated. Instead of being an aid to Paul, Epaphroditus became a hindrance and a burden in his illness. Then, when he finally recovered, recognizing that his imprisonment was soon to end, Paul was able to send him back to Philippi.[271] Martin argues for this "double commission" on Epaphroditus from the Philippian church based on Paul's commendation in Philippians 2:28.[272] Craddock also sees him playing a double role but understands his commission from the church to be for an indefinite length of time, such that his return was sooner than desired or expected. He further sees a part of Paul's motive for sending him back to Philippi as "an act which will relieve Paul

---

269 Martin, *Philippians*, 121.
270 Beare, *Philippians*, 99.
271 Lenski, Galatians, Ephesians, Philippians, 818-25.
272 Martin, *Philippians*, 122.

(he is in no position to wait upon the sick), the church (which has heard of Epaphroditus' illness), and Epaphroditus himself (who has been distressed that the church was distressed)."[273] This view sees Paul's comments concerning Epaphroditus as serving to smooth away any possible criticisms for his supposedly failing to represent them well in their desire to aid Paul. This would accommodate the idea that Epaphroditus was homesick rather than vexed over the anxiety of his home church. But it places Paul in a position of crediting Epaphroditus with stronger character. Paul's commendation indicates that homesickness is not a strong possibility for Epaphroditus' illness.

What was his role with respect to Paul? Paul clearly had other believers, as evidenced by his closing comments in the letter to the Philippians (Phil 4:21). At least Luke and some others can be located with him in Rome based on Luke's reference to "we" in Acts 28:16. Paul's first imprisonment does not appear to have been a severe experience, especially since he was permitted to entertain visitors at will while remaining under house arrest (Acts 28:30-31).[274] Even so, Epaphroditus had come to him as more than a courier, but rather someone to remain with him and serve a useful purpose.

This raises the question of his condition when he was returned to his home church. It is not possible to know how well he was when he returned. It would suffice to say that, in light of travel conditions in those days, if he were well enough to travel from Rome to Philippi, he would certainly be well enough to return to serving Paul. Thus, his being sent home did not have a secret or secondary purpose of removing a liability as Craddock views it, but rather a desire to remove anxiety on the parts of both Epaphroditus and the church in Philippi.[275] Lightfoot ex-

---

273 Craddock, "Philippians," 51.
274 Stephen L. Belch, "Paul's Life After the Close of Acts," (ThM thesis, DTS, 1982) 78.
275 Motyer, *Philippians*, 143.

plains this interpretation of the evidence well. "He was oppressed with the thought that the Philippians would have heard of his critical state. He was anxious to return that he might quiet their alarm."[276] Paul was likewise anxious for him to return so that their anxiety could be calmed, and Paul would not feel responsible for their having to endure any further worry (Phil 2:28).

Paul's inability to heal

One might argue from Paul's sending Epaphroditus back that he really did not need his services and thus had no need to heal him. Yet Paul's response of distress at his near-death reveals that, whether needed or not, Paul in no way wanted to see him expire. Thus, Paul's inability to heal can be argued based on his horror at the possible death of this committed fellow worker and his admission that God spared his life. The inference is also that Paul could not offer healing assistance at this time. Otherwise, it would have been a simple matter to heal him by exercising his apostolic authority. Collange, commenting on the question of faith healing, observes, "Paul says nothing about resorting to any thaumaturgic activities: he mentions neither faith nor prayer nor the laying on of hands any more than he does the effect of medicines or of a doctor."[277] Thus, though he was disturbed greatly by the illness, there is no indication of an attempt to effect a supernatural cure.

Assuming his illness resulted from the trip to Rome, it had to last enough time so that his companions would have completed their visit and felt compelled to return to Philippi while still unsure of their friend's recovery. On the other hand, if it resulted from exhaustion, it might be expected that Philippi had heard from people other than their own company about his difficulty. It is interesting to note that if he had fallen ill near his arrival,

---

276 Lightfoot, *Philippians*, 62.
277 Jean-Francois Collange, *The Epistle of Saint Paul to the Philippians*, 121. Wilkinson (*Health and Healing*, 110) agrees with this observation.

the other companions of Epaphroditus would have left him in the hands of an apostle who, if he could still heal people as he had done in their church a few years earlier, would be expected to intervene on behalf of their companion. Yet they would have then left knowing that he was still critically ill, thus knowing that Paul either would not or could not heal. Further, assuming he became ill after the other Philippians had returned home and word reached Philippi through subsequent communications, unless they already knew that miracles had passed away, upon hearing of his illness, they would naturally have been unconcerned since they would not expect Paul to allow him to expire. Epaphroditus' anxiety in response to the report of their anxiety reveals that they had no such expectation. Based on his comments concerning his anxiety about Epaphroditus, it must be concluded that he could not heal him rather than would not. The attitudes of both Paul and the Philippians indicate a general understanding in the church that by this point in history, miracles, even at the hands of apostles, was not an expected event. It appears that all Paul could do was pray for him and hope God would keep him from death.

In response to the belief that Epaphroditus argues against miracle healings, Duffield and Van Cleave consider him as an example supporting miracle healing. They understand Paul's statement that "God had mercy on him" (Phil 2:26) to refer to miraculous intervention by God.[278] The weakness of this response is that it does not address why Paul himself was unable to heal him. Also, the text does not refer to God's mercy upon him as coming from miraculous intervention but simply a sparing of his life. Though the verse could allow for miraculous healing, the tenor of the passage and Paul's expressed relief at his survival argue for a non-miraculous recovery.

---

278 Duffield and Van Cleave, Foundations of Pentecostal Theology, 411.

Timothy

Timothy was one of Paul's earlier companions and representatives. He joined Paul on his second missionary journey and was later described by him as one who served with him in the furtherance of the gospel as a child serving his father (Phil 2:19-22). Thus they had a very intimate fellowship, shared purpose and attitude in ministry.[279] Bruce observes that "Timothy readily surrendered whatever personal ambitions he might have cherished in order to play the part of a son to Paul and help him in his missionary activity, showing a selfless concern for others that matched the apostle's own eagerness to spend and be spent for them."[280] Paul described him as his fellow worker (Rom 16:21), mentioned him as a fellow author of his epistles (Phil 1:1; Col 1:1; 1 Thess 1:1; 2 Thess 1:1; and Phlm 1), and used him as a messenger to the churches (Acts 19:22; 1 Cor 4:17, 16:10; Phil 2:19; and 1 Thess 3:2, 6). His letters to Timothy also show the closeness of their relationship and the importance of Timothy to Paul. They also reveal the challenges, stresses, and depth of responsibilities Timothy faced as pastor of the church in Ephesus. He was a person in need of all his physical resources to accomplish his purpose in the church.

His place in the timeline

Though he had been with him frequently over many years, Paul's mention of Timothy's illness comes in his first letter to Timothy, which was written following his first Roman imprisonment while he was again moving freely through the Roman world. This being the only mention of the illness, it is impossible to say with certainty whether he had always had difficulties or developed them later. It is clear, though, that by the writing of 1 Timothy, they could be referred to as "frequent ailments" (1 Tim 5:23).

---

279 Robert Rainy, *The Epistle to the Philippians*, The Expositor's Bible (New York: Hodder & Stoughton, n.d.) 158.

280 Bruce, 1 and 2 Thessalonians, 457.

APOSTOLIC *Signs and Gifts* OF THE SPIRIT

The circumstances and nature of his illness

Timothy's illness, related to his stomach (or intestines), was chronic. Wilkinson identified his illness as probably a chronic achlorphydric dyspepsia, which would produce disabling attacks on his health.[281] Vine understood Paul's instructions to Timothy not to drink water exclusively to indicate he had taken up a lifestyle of at least partial asceticism, which may have left him open to ingesting contaminated water. He argues that the "exacting character of Timothy's labours [sic] and the heavy responsibilities devolving upon him, with all the antecedent trials and perils in his missionary activities, no doubt had a prejudicial effect upon his health (there is no evidence that Timothy was constitutionally a weakling previous to his call to such work). He had evidently confined himself to the use of water for drinking, perhaps with the godly desire to set an example against the evils of intoxication prevalent in Ephesus."[282] Barclay also argues for the possibility of asceticism based on his mother being a Jewess from whom he could have learned such a view of piety.[283] Considering the statement by Paul concerning his coming to faith and the role both his mother and grandmother had in his upbringing (2 Tim 1:5), it is very likely indeed that his heritage of a "sincere faith" was from the pietistic element of his Jewish background. Since the drinking water of that day was of questionable purity at best, avoiding water that had been "treated" with a mixture of wine would expose him to frequent intestinal difficulties. This would explain then Paul's advice to use the wine medicinally. Gromacki argues this position based on the use of the preposition "for" (*dia*), which "introduces two reasons for the medicinal use of wine. First, Timothy had a weak stomach ('for thy stomach's sake'). . . . Second, he had 'often infirmities.' . . . He had

---

281 Wilkinson, *Health and Healing*, 110.
282 W. E. Vine, *The Epistles to Timothy and Titus* (Grand Rapids: Zondervan, 1965), 88.
283 William Barclay, *The Letters to Timothy, Titus, and Philemon*, rev. ed. (Philadelphia: Westminster Press, 1975), 119.

many 'infirmities' (note the plural) and he had them 'often.'"[284] Thus, Timothy was plagued by a continuing problem that could only hinder his ministry.

His "frequent ailments" would have had to persist over several months or years before this comment by Paul. This would indicate the opportunity for contact with Paul while he had this condition. Hoehner's chronology shows Paul in contact with Timothy on at least two occasions between his arrival in Rome and his first epistle to Timothy.[285] Therefore there was no lack of opportunity to alleviate his suffering involved in its continuance. Paul was physically present with him. Further, based on Paul's experience in Ephesus, he should have had the authority to heal from a distance. He could have simply prayed for Timothy's healing, and it would have happened.

Paul's need to heal

Timothy was an integral part of Paul's ministry and very important to him as an assistant. Lockyer describes his relationship to Paul by exclaiming, "How indispensable he became to the apostle (Acts 17:14, 15: 18:5; 20:4)! Paul had no other companion so 'like-minded' as Timothy, who enjoyed Paul's constant instruction (Tim 2:3; 3:14)."[286] Later, he left Timothy in charge of the church in Ephesus while he was still traveling. Yet in his first letter to him, while he had the burden of leadership, he did not offer to heal Timothy's infirmity but rather told him to take medicinal measures to alleviate some of the misery.

Paul's inability to heal

Having established that Paul had opportunities to heal Timothy and had expressed the desire to see him in full health, it is apparent that Paul found himself unable to help his favorite son in

---

284 Robert G. Gromacki, *Stand True to the Charge* (Grand Rapids: Baker Book House, 1982), 153.
285 Heohner, "Chronology of the Apostolic Age," 338-40.
286 Lockyer, *All the Men of the Bible* (Grand Rapids: Zondervan, 1958), 329.

the ministry. Of interest is Paul's failure to tell him to call for a healer or offer to heal at their next meeting. He also did not tell him to follow the instructions of James (Jas 5:14-15). Paul did not address a sin problem. Nor did he say that healing was not for believers or leaders. There is no explanation or offer of any but medicinal hope for Timothy.

One might argue that it was not a life-threatening disease but only a cause of discomfort and so did not deserve apostolic intervention. It might be further argued that these frequent debilitating illnesses served as Timothy's "thorn in the flesh," and so Paul either would not or could not intervene on his behalf. The absence of any statement by Paul in this regard makes such a theory very tenuous at best. Further, the advice given to take medicinal measures to alleviate suffering would argue against such conclusions since the effect of the wine was expected to be beneficial to his stomach. Paul's affliction was given to him by God directly due to the revelations he had been privileged to receive and the danger of resulting pride. Thus, the goal of maintaining Paul's humility was clearly in view as stated by him in 2 Corinthians 12:7-9. Timothy appears to have suffered more from timidity than pride, so no need for a similar thorn can be demonstrated. Stott remarks that "Paul is fully alert to the difficulties, however, both internal and external. Timothy himself is inexperienced, infirm and shy."[287]

The weight of responsibility left to Timothy by Paul, on the other hand, would argue for a very real need, even desirability, for Timothy's health to be maintained. Further, Paul's instruction to take a little wine and not drink water exclusively shows his expressed desire for Timothy's health to improve and maintain. Paul is unmistakably concerned for his well-being. Thus, it is legitimate to say that Paul, desiring his health if he could have

---

[287] John R. W. Stott, *Guard the Gospel: The Message of 2 Timothy* (Downers Grove: InterVarsity Press, 1973), 126.

healed him, would have healed him. It appears that healing was simply not an option at this point in history.

Trophimus

Trophimus the Ephesian first appears as a companion of Paul on his third missionary journey, being listed as a member of his company who was sent ahead and awaited his arrival in Troas as he made his way to Jerusalem (Acts 20:4-6). He was, therefore, a witness of Paul's raising Eutychus from the dead at Troas (Acts 20:7-12). Later, he was seen publicly with Paul in Jerusalem and is one of the Greeks Paul was accused of taking into the temple (Acts 21:27-29). Thus, his place as a member of Paul's ministry team and a companion is established from the record of Acts. He was not again named in the remainder of Acts but may have well been one of the men who accompanied Paul to Rome and may possibly be included with Luke in the "we" statements of Acts 27 and 28. He is lastly mentioned in Paul's second letter to Timothy (2 Tim 4:20), which was written shortly before his execution in Rome.

His place in the timeline

The evidence points to a late date for Trophimus' illness in relation to Paul's life and ministry. Second Timothy, in which Trophimus' illness is mentioned, was written near the end of Paul's ministry soon after his re-imprisonment in Rome. During his final travels, he passed through Miletus around the fall of AD 66.[288] Paul must have traveled through Miletus soon before his second Roman arrest.[289] Trophimus was likely left at Miletus while Paul was a prisoner on his way to Rome the second time and thus accompanied him partway there before falling ill.[290] Woychuk places him very near Paul's imprisonment but does not state

---

288 Hoehner, "Chronology of the Apostolic Age," 347-48.
289 Stephen L. Belch, "Paul's Life After the Close of Acts" (ThM thesis, DTS, 1982), 73-74.
290 Stott, Guard the Gospel, 118.

whether Paul was still free or a prisoner.[291] From the record of 2 Timothy, whether he was left just before Paul's arrest or while en route to Rome the second time, his placement chronologically is significant in that it locates him at a critical time in Paul's ministry. It was a time when his friends and helpers were either being separated from him by necessity or were deserting him.

The Circumstances and nature of his illness
Paul's report to Timothy concerning Trophimus provides scant information about either the circumstances or the nature of his illness. All that is known is that it occurred when Paul was experiencing desertion and was sending key men to key cities. Paul reported to Timothy that Demas had deserted him (2 Tim 4:10) and that all the rest of his companions except Luke had gone to other cities, presumably being left or sent by Paul (2 Tim 4:10-12, 20). Then he mentioned Trophimus, whom he had left sick at Miletus. Though no indication is given of the exact ailment, his illness was of such severity that Trophimus could not continue with Paul on his travels and had to be left behind.

Paul's need to heal
Trophimus' illness is reported in the same time frame as the departures of faithful men and desertions of others from Paul's company. It came when Paul could not afford to be unnecessarily losing additional men from his company. Thus, if Paul had the ability at that time to heal, he logically and of necessity would have exercised it.

The pattern of Paul's ministry was to work through a team of men. This is reflected in the "we" passages of Acts and the groups of names he associated with himself in his epistles. There were times when he moved on journeys alone. However, he was always rejoined at a predetermined location by one or more key

---

291 N. A. Woychuk, *Exposition of Second Timothy* (St. Louis: Miracle Press, 1973), 170.

men.²⁹² Though he continued without Trophimus, the pattern is that Paul preferred the company and assistance of others in his ministry. Stott correctly understood the tenor of 2 Timothy 4 to indicate a real desire on Paul's part to have someone with him during his final days. "Nevertheless, the apostle feels himself terribly cut off and abandoned, exiled from the churches he founded and from the people in them he knows and loves. More poignant still is the fact that a number of his close circle of travelling companions have—for a variety of reasons—left him or become separated from him. It is their fellowship that he misses more than anybody's."²⁹³ Hiebert commented on Paul's uncomfortable circumstances. "Paul explains the absence of two companions whom Timothy would expect to be with Paul." He then pointed out that Paul further remarked that Trophimus had been left behind.²⁹⁴ The inference then was that Paul would have expected to have others traveling with him, and their absence was noteworthy. 2 Timothy 4:11 shows that only Luke was with Paul in Rome. Thus, the loss of a companion, especially if he was en route to Rome as a prisoner at the time, would sorely hurt Paul. He had very good reason to want to keep Trophimus healthy if he could. This is further seen in his request for Timothy to come to him and bring John Mark, who could be "very useful" to Paul.²⁹⁵

Paul's inability to heal
Though there is very little information provided in Scripture, the inference concerning this last companion of Paul's to fall ill is that Paul could do nothing to help him. Booth observes that "Paul exercised the gift of miracles frequently in his missionary

---

292 For example, Paul possibly went from Berea to Athens alone, where he then awaited the arrival of Silas and Timothy (Acts 17:15-16). He further moved on to Corinth before he was finally joined by them there (Acts 18:1, 5).
293 Stott, Guard the Gospel, 118.
294 D. Edmond Hiebert, *Second Timothy* (Chicago: Moody Press, 1958), 124.
295 Stott, Guard the Gospel, 119.

travels, but in his later years Paul was unable to heal Trophimus whom he left at Miletus sick (2 Tim 4:20)."[296] Lockyer also raises this issue by saying that the "apostle who had the gift of healing could do nothing for his sick friend—a fact quack faith healers should note."[297] Though this incident offers difficulties for those holding to modern faith healing, still the question raised is whether this non-healing is evidence showing that apostolic authority did not include freedom to act apart from the direction of God, a loss of earlier ability had been experienced, or something else is indicated. Duffield and Van Cleave respond to the argument for an end to miraculous healers from the example of Trophimus by saying that "healing is not always instantaneous."[298] This response is weak since there is only one non-instantaneous healing recorded in the New Testament. Jesus healed a man born blind in two steps in Mark 8:22-26. Though there was a minute or two between Jesus' spitting on his eyes and then the man's full restoration, the second step in his healing brought instant relief. Thus, Paul's leaving behind Trophimus must be explained more adequately before his example can be ignored by proponents of modern miracle healing.

Some have understood Paul's failure to heal Trophimus to indicate that his healings were occasional and only at God's discretion rather than performable at his own will. Woychuk sees the leaving of Trophimus while sick as an indication that even apostles could not heal at will but that they were exceptional manifestations of power.[299] Vine understood it to indicate that the apostles were subject to God's choices. "Whilst such supernatural gifts were bestowed to confirm the work of the gospel, there were limitations as to its exercise. The Apostles' use of the gift was not directed by their own wishes. They were acting sim-

---

[296] Booth, "The Purpose of Miracles" 203.
[297] Lockyer, All the Miracles of the Bible, 332.
[298] Duffield and Van Cleave, *Foundations*, 411.
[299] Woychuk, *Second Timothy*, 170.

ply as the Lord's servants and their power was controlled by their Master, and not by their personal affections or desires. The healing was accomplished by faith, but faith-healing was not practiced as an art."[300]

The evidence of Paul's raising Eutychus along with his extraordinary ministry in Ephesus argues against this view. Concerning Eutychus in Acts 20:7-12, though the youth was not a part of his company, Paul immediately raised him from the dead. There is no indication that he consulted God in this matter or had any doubt that his attempt would fail. Rather, his quick reaction to the circumstances shows that at that point in his ministry, he had the ability, at will and on the spur of the moment, to effect great miracles even when authentication of his apostleship was not an issue, and no unbelievers were present to view the manifested power of God. Similarly, the extraordinary miracles God was performing by the hand of Paul in Ephesus included the sending out of aprons and handkerchiefs to the sick who were then healed on contact with the cloths (Acts 19:11-12). Bruce and Longenecker both argue for the people's faith being the cause of their healing rather than any power lodged within the pieces of cloth themselves.[301] This would seem to direct attention away from Paul as the miracle worker, focusing on Luke's account of his ministry in Ephesus. The text points toward the demonstrated power of Paul to effect healing even from a distance. The cloths leaving his person were no longer under his control, yet Scripture indicates that those who touched them were healed. The picture then is of Paul wielding great authority and being able to heal even at random as well as at will. This is also the picture of Peter when the people were healed simply by his shadow passing over them (Acts 5:12-16).[302] As Bruce

---

300 Vine, *Timothy and Titus*, 150.
301 Bruce, *1 and 2 Thessalonians*, 292; Richard N. Longenecker, "The Acts of the Apostles," *The Expositor's Bible Commentary*, vol. 9 (Grand Rapids: Zondervan Publishing House, 1981), 496.
302 Ibid., 317.

notes well, "Peter's shadow was as efficacious a medium of healing power as the hem of his Master's robe had been."[303] Granted, the people were exercising faith, yet their faith was useless apart from Peter's shadow passing over them. Again, as with Paul, it was not he who was determining the beneficiaries, but those fortunate enough to position themselves placed along his path. Further, when Peter arrived in Joppa, he raised Dorcas from the dead with only believers present and at will (Acts 9:36-43). Thus, the picture painted of both Peter and Paul in the record of Acts does not indicate that there were any limitations on their miracle-working abilities at the beginning of their ministries. And, even on Malta near the end of Paul's period of working miracles, he healed all who came to him and showed no sign of limitation (Acts 28:7-10).

Summary

In summary, we see evidence from the experience of three of Paul's companions that Paul appears to have been unable to heal them. There does not appear to be any reason to leave any of them in their state of illness. Rather, there was every reason to intercede on their behalf. We must conclude that Paul could not heal them, not that he chose not to heal them.

Church History

In his book, *Charismatic Gifts in the Early Church*, Ronald Kydd reported his findings on the expression of the gift of prophecy within the church during the first two centuries. What he found was a church that began "strongly charismatic" till around AD 200, followed by a loss of interest over the next 50 years. He notes then that, after AD 260 any evidence of "charismatic experience" disappears. He searched the literature until AD 320, the limit of

---

303 Bruce, *The Book of the Acts*, NICNT (Grand Rapids: William B. Eerdmans, n.d.), 118.

his research, and found consistent silence.³⁰⁴ A good summary of his findings can be seen in this assessment by him "Throughout the first and second century, Christians enjoyed the presence of the gifts of the Spirit in their worship. ... However, following about AD 260 evidence for the presence of spiritual gifts is non-existent. It looks as though by then they had ceased to be a part of the day-by-day experience of the Christians of the time. This means that the block of time from ca. 200 to 260 is a transitional period as far as the gifts of the Spirit were concerned."³⁰⁵

The testimony of John Chrysostom (ca. 347-407) confirms this. He writes concerning the spiritual gifts, "This whole place is very obscure: but the obscurity is produced by our ignorance of the facts referred to and by their cessation, being such as then used to occur but now no longer take place."³⁰⁶

Kydd focused on the spiritual gift of prophecy rather than healing. In addition, he looked at the *Didache* and noted that it gives us insight into the church during the latter half of the first century.³⁰⁷ The *Didache* contained discussions about how to discern between true and false prophets and addressed the question of prophecy.³⁰⁸ He notes that prophecy continued to be "highly valued" in the churches and those he identifies as "charismatics" were clearly active in the churches at that time. From this, he concludes, "The Syrian communities to which the *Didache* was written sometime between AD 50 and 100 were very much aware of the ministry of spiritual gifts, and they were not alone."³⁰⁹ Clement of Rome refers to "spiritual gifts" being exercised in the

---

304 Ronald A. N. Kydd, *Charismatic Gifts in the Early Church* (Peabody, MA: Hendrickson, 1984), 4.
305 Ibid., 57.
306 John Chrysostom, *Homilies on First Corinthians*, 1 Cor. 12:1,2, in *Saint Chrysostom: Homilies on the Epistles of Paul to the Corinthians*, ed. Philip Schaff, trans. Hubert Kestell Cornish, John Medley, and Talbot B. Chambers, vol. 12, A Select Library of the Nicene and Post-Nicene Fathers of the Christian Church, First Series (New York: Christian Literature Company, 1889), 168.
307 Ibid., 6.
308 Ibid., 8.
309 Ibid., 11.

church in *1 Clement* 38:1.[310] Ignatius of Antioch (early second century) is believed by him to have been both an "administrator" and a prophet in his church.[311] Kydd notes further, "If how you decide whether a prophet is true or false was an issue there must have been a fair number of prophets around."[312] Further, at the time Justin Martyr wrote his *Dialogue with Trypho* (between AD 162 and 168), spiritual gifts were still very evident in the church.[313] However, as noted earlier, the presence of these gifts ceased to be mentioned by the middle of the third century. They had passed from the scene.

Kydd, in the introduction to his book, identifies himself as a Pentecostal and expressed his surprise at his findings. The significance of his findings is that they can be an indication that all miraculous gifts disappeared as the church matured and needed them less. It must be noted that these gifts passed from the scene while the church was still experiencing persecution from the Roman government. Persecution did not keep the church from growing into a mature body in these early years. And, it appears, with that growing maturity came a lessening need for the supernatural manifestations of the Spirit. His assessment is insightful. "The church underwent many changes during the first two and one-half centuries of its life. ... The Christian community grew phenomenally in size; it became increasingly wealthy; it climbed the social ladder; its level of education rose; it developed its organization, and it formalized its worship. While all this was going on, the gifts of the Spirit just quietly slipped away. Perhaps no one really noticed it happening. Certainly, no one felt concerned

---

[310] "Let our whole body, then, be preserved in, Christ Jesus; and let every one [sic] be subject to his neighbour, according to the special gift bestowed upon him." (Clement of Rome, "The First Epistle of Clement to the Corinthians," in *The Apostolic Fathers with Justin Martyr and Irenaeus*, ed. Alexander Roberts, James Donaldson, and A. Cleveland Coxe, The Ante-Nicene Fathers, vol. 1 [Buffalo, NY: Christian Literature Company, 1885], 15.)

[311] Kydd, Charismatic Gifts in the Early Church, 18.

[312] Ibid., 20.

[313] Ibid., 27-28.

enough to take the trouble to try and stop the trend. The gifts just disappeared. The crucial time was the early part of the third century."[314] But can we see hints of its beginning even in the first century? That may be an explanation for what happened with the Apostle Paul.

---

314 Ibid., 57.

6

Paul's Inability

To Heal

Its Significance

The evidence of these three close associates of Paul whose illnesses were left to their natural courses points to an inability to heal on Paul's part. Though the evidence of Scripture regarding these men does not *conclusively* prove a loss of ability, it implies that loss. Ryrie interprets the evidence with more certitude when he says, "There is obviously a phasing out of some of the miracles in the life of the one who performed them. Paul had the gift of healing, but he must have lost it or not have been able to exercise it after a certain time."[315] Whitcomb agrees with Ryrie, seeing the miracles' purpose as having been completed. He says:

> Paul's last recorded miracles were performed on the island of Malta, one of which was a remarkable fulfillment of our Lord's promise to the apostles that they would not be hurt by deadly serpents (Acts 28:1-10; Mark 16:18). But after Paul arrived in Rome, his miracle-working powers

---

315 Ryrie, "Miracles (or What Happened to Your Handkerchiefs, Paul?)," 83.

were apparently withdrawn by the Lord. ... Thus, step by step, God was removing the scaffolding of miracles from the early church as the New Testament Scriptures were being completed and the apostles and prophets were dying off.[316]

To confirm such conclusions, the question of Paul's friends' non-healings must be further discussed. Either Paul could and chose not to heal them, or he was helpless with regard to their conditions. To justify a position that Paul chose not to heal them, one must demonstrate logically that either they were not essential men in his ministry or that he would view their suffering as "fulfilling that which was lacking in Christ's afflictions" (Gal 2:24f) even as he viewed his own sufferings. That Timothy's suffering was not a "thorn" like Paul's has been discussed already. With respect to essentiality, the case of Timothy might be argued in terms of his illness not affecting Paul directly and his being able to continue directing the church at Ephesus from a bed, but not Trophimus or Epaphroditus. Their illnesses came at times when their services were badly needed. It would not be strategic for Paul to weaken his team by eliminating key personnel, especially if he had the ability to simply speak the word or touch them and restore them to full health. His deliverance of Eutychus from death shows his willingness to restore even those who were not essential to his ministry. It is also evident that Paul could exercise the option at will, even when he was not being watched by an unbelieving audience. Thus, the miracle did not have to be directly related to authentication of the message or messenger, since the recipient and viewers of this miracle were all supporters of Paul's apostleship. They already recognized his authority.

---

316 John C. Whitcomb, Jr. "Does God Want Christians to Perform Miracles Today?" *Grace Journal* 12: 3 (Fall 1971): 8.

A possible explanation for Paul not healing his friends might be based on healing being only for non-believers in areas where the gospel was first preached.[317] This concept is presently being propagated to argue for modern miracles working in conjunction with gospel preaching to unreached tribal groups.[318] Again, Eutychus' restoration by Paul devastates such an option. Paul's inference in 2 Corinthians concerning his ability to demonstrate his apostolic authority must have included an ability to heal believers since that authority mentioned was to be demonstrated before the congregation of believers and not for the sake of unbelievers. Also, Peter's raising of Dorcas, a believer, shows that other apostles readily aided believers. Lastly, the gifts of healing in Corinthians shows that at least in the early days of the church believers could expect to find release from their illnesses. Thus, one cannot argue that healings and signs were for unbelievers only.

To argue that each of the three men either lacked faith or had unresolved sins is not acceptable either. They had each been with Paul on his missionary journeys and had seen him performing signs and wonders, including healings. There is no rational reason to expect them to then doubt Paul's ability. As eyewitnesses, rather, one would expect them to ask for Paul's intervention on their behalf. Further, Paul's references to Epaphroditus in his letter to the Philippians presents the picture of a man of faith, courage, and commitment rather than of sin or faithlessness. Yet, Epaphroditus nearly died. It is impossible to argue for a lack of faith. Thus, some other answer must be sought.

When the circumstances are reviewed, especially for Epaphroditus and Trophimus, their need, as well as Paul's, requires one to conclude that Paul had to lack the ability to intervene. Other-

---

317 This is not an attempt to raise "straw man" arguments, but to look at what could be considered legitimate arguments someone might make.
318 David Clark, "Miracles Lead to Revivals," *Christian Life* 44: 7 (November 1982): 34; De Wet, "Biblical Basis of Signs and Wonders," 33; Wagner, "Signs & Wonders: What difference do they make?" *Christian Life* 44: 7 (November 1982): 78.

wise, their suffering and his loss of their assistance were needless. From this we can then say that we have evidence of a decline in miracles even within the experience of the apostles who were the principal miracle workers of the church.

Argument from Silence

The majority of evidence which men have to draw from Scripture concerning the question of miracles continuing or declining unfortunately does not include direct statements. Rather, it comes from circumstantial evidence in locations that do not address the question of miracles and so forces extrapolation. Yet, adequate evidence is provided within God's providence to allow an opportunity for analysis. Even so, this has led to the propagation of many positions concerning the possibility of modern miracle workers, with the faith healing proponents claiming to have performed miraculous cures and reporting resurrections and healings in faraway places where confirmation is nearly impossible. From these testimonies has developed their insistence that God is performing as many miracles today as He did in the first century. They argue further that those proposing that miracles did not continue beyond the first century are guilty of limiting God and ignoring an important element of the gospel taught in Scripture.[319]

Arguing any theological position based on the silences of Scripture is tenuous at best. Thiessen points out that "the argument from silence never settles a question conclusively."[320] This is true concerning the question of the continuance or cessation of miracles. Miller affirms that there are no texts of Scripture that state categorically that miracles were to continue.[321] MacArthur

---

[319] Peder Borgen, "Miracles of Healing in the New Testament," 91; Cavnar, "Miracles: Do They Really Happen?," 5; De Wet, "Biblical Basis of Signs and Wonders," 28; Taylor, "Miracles—Yes or No?" 9.
[320] Thiessen, *Introduction*, 300.
[321] Wayman D. Miller, *Modern Divine Healing*, 303.

goes further to state, "Nothing in Scripture indicates that the things that occurred during the apostolic age are to occur in subsequent ages. Nor does the Bible exhort the believer to seek any miraculous manifestations of the Holy Spirit."[322] Taylor, on the other hand, understands the same silence as arguing for their continuance. He says, "Without becoming tedious over passages that everyone knows full well, it can be rather categorically stated that the New Testament simply does not affirm that the Church should expect God to stop working miracles among His people."[323] Further, Duffield and Van Cleave respond to the claims of miracles ceasing by asking, "Where is the statement in the Bible that miracles would cease to be performed?"[324] The New Testament is more silent on the issue than spoken, forcing advocates of either position to search long for any evidence which might point to a solution. Still, though it is silent regarding any teachings concerning the use and abuse of miracles in the church, the New Testament record is not completely silent with respect to the presence or absence of miracles. It only becomes silent in those writings which follow Paul's Roman imprisonment.[325]

The silence of Scripture has been used by opponents of the modern faith healing movement to argue forcefully for an end to miracles through miracle workers. For example, Hillis considers the silence of the latter epistles as strong evidence concerning the cessation of miracles in the church and gives a warning against granting miracles more significance than they appear to have attained in the first days of the church. Regarding the gift of healing, he says:

---

[322] MacArthur, Jr., *The Charismatics*, 76.
[323] Taylor, "Miracles—Yes or No?," 9.
[324] Duffield and Van Cleave, *Foundations*, 406.
[325] Miller, Modern Divine Healing, 317.

It is not without import that Peter and John never refer to the subject in their epistles. Paul completely omits it in his long letter to the Romans. He never mentions it in his second letter to the Corinthians. In the rest of his wonderful prison epistles he doesn't so much as allude to the "gifts of healing." He gives no instruction in his pastoral letters on the subject. And whoever may have written the letter to the Hebrews failed to bring up the matter of healing.[326]

The very silence of these God-inspired writers relative to the subject of the "gifts of healing" should warn us of the danger of making much of that which God makes little. Booth agrees with him and uses Peter as a model of the decline. He says,

> If the gift of miracles was a permanent gift, one would expect to find it exercised with some degree of regularity throughout the lifetime of an individual possessing the gift. But even a casual reading of the New Testament reveals that the gift of miracles gradually faded from prominence among the men who earlier possessed the gift. Peter made great use of miracles in the early years of the church, but when he wrote his two epistles thirty years later, he does not even make mention of miracles.[327]

Edgar points to the silences of several epistles as well as Paul's letter to the Galatians to argue against the place of miracles in the modern church. He says first concerning the Galatians:

> The problem of the Galatians was not solved by an appeal to spiritual gifts, but by an appeal to sound doctrine and to act in Christian love. There is no intimation that some who possessed certain gifts had an advantage in this re-

---

326 Hillis, *Tongues, Healing, and You!*, Section 2, 28.
327 Booth, "The Purpose of Miracles," 202.

gard, but rather that all were exhorted to be sound in doctrine and to love one another. [328]

Then, with regard to those epistles written during or after Paul's imprisonment in Rome, he says:

> Spiritual gifts are not a part of the armor that the individual needs to stand against Satan and his wiles. ... There are no mentions of spiritual gifts in the book of Philippians, although there are numerous admonitions to love and spirituality. The same applies to Colossians. ... First Peter, which is written to believers undergoing trials, has much to say regarding the Christian life, but the only mention of gifts concerns ministry to others.[329]

Without the presence of the three friends of Paul and the statement of Hebrews 2:3-4, the debate concerning the continuance or cessation of miracles, including tongues and healing, could never be more than an argument from silence for both positions. Yet, those who wish to press for a continuance of miracles through the apostolic period into the present must explain Paul's failure to heal his friends and assistants in the ministry. Though their continued illnesses are not a direct statement that miracles had completely ended, they do force examination of any claim to their continuance. Their non-healings evidence either an inability or unwillingness to heal on Paul's part. Booth points to this evidence to build his argument for an end to miracles. He says:

> Paul exercised the gift of miracles frequently in his missionary travels, but in his later years Paul was unable to heal Trophimus whom he left at Miletus sick (2 Tim. 4:20). In addition, Paul tells of Epaphroditus being sick

---
328 Edgar, Miraculous Gifts: Are They for Today? 38.
329 Ibid., 39-41.

nigh unto death (Phil. 2:26-27), recommends a medical remedy to Timothy (1 Tim. 5:23), and was unable to remove the infirmity that plagued himself (2 Cor. 12:7). Had Paul still possessed the gift of miracles, it seems that he certainly would have healed some of these cases of sickness. While the exact moment of the cessation of the gift of miracles cannot be declared dogmatically, it can be said that the gift did fade away gradually, and that by the end of the apostolic era (ca. A.D. 100), it had ceased completely.[330]

The similar silence of other portions of Scripture regarding miracles and miracle workers is used by men to argue for other periods of inactivity on God's part. For example, Forge argues:

> It is very obvious that the great mass of Biblical miracles are grouped in a very few cycles, while long stretches of Bible history are as free of the marvelous as any rationalistic critic could demand. ... The Old Testament miracles gather largely around two periods of time which are either centered in a new divine order which was being set up or a time of national emergency. ... Long periods of Old Testament history were devoid of the miraculous and only in times of great need did God stretch forth His hand to perform wonders.[331]

He then draws from this pattern the conclusion that God should not be expected to continue working miracles indefinitely.

The miracles, though of some impact, were never an emphasis of the apostolic ministry in the sense that they were not ends in and of themselves. The gospel was of primary importance. It was not miracles which drew men to Christ, but the Holy Spirit working through the message of salvation. The Apostle Paul did

---

330 Booth, "The Purpose of Miracles," 202-203.
331 Forge, "The Doctrine of Miracles in the Apostolic Church," 17-19.

not point his readers to miracles as the key to the conversions of men but rather that "faith comes from hearing, and hearing by the word of Christ" (Rom 10:17). Their usefulness came only in their relationship to their authentication of the apostolic messenger, such as can be seen in 2 Corinthians 12:12. It would naturally follow that, even during the time of miracle-working they would not obtain much attention from the apostles. As a result, only possible hints of them are seen in Paul's journey epistles, and then only when being used apologetically as evidence of God's working. In Galatians 2 Paul refers to the experience of miracles in their midst as proof that they received the Spirit by faith and not by the works of the Law. In 2 Corinthians 12:12 he uses the evidence of his own miracle-working to argue for his apostleship. But, even before that, in his first epistle to the Corinthian church, before discussing the gifts of the Spirit and their misuse in that church, he does not point to his own miracle-working power as proof of his apostleship, but to the lives of the people to whom he was writing. This being true, their decline and cessation would not be expected to elicit any significant attention. The silence could be understood then, not as the result of embarrassment at their loss or as the consequence of their commonness but as the result of a consistent non-emphasis of miracles in light of the greater need of the average, non-miracle-working Christian of their day to understand the gospel and to live righteously, by faith and not by sight, before their God.

In conclusion, though silence alone is a weak argument, the consistent silences of key portions of Scripture, combined with evidence that healings were not accomplished at critical times by the very one who could send out handkerchiefs earlier, demands an explanation. To argue that the lack of any direct statement to the effect that miracles had ended is necessary before one can conclude their cessation flies in the face of the indications of the historical references within the epistolary literature which followed Paul's imprisonment. Therefore, though silence alone is a weak argument, silence combined with other evidence becomes a support for the position that miracles through miracle workers ended within the first century. Further, when the evidence is understood in light of the theological purpose of miracles, it becomes stronger support for miracles ceasing.

Argument for Purpose

A strong argument for the purpose of miracles being the authentication of the apostolic messengers has been made. This provides a very plausible explanation for both the early non-emphasis of miracles in the apostolic literature and the later silence concerning them in the epistles. Also, it explains the relationship that Paul's three unhealed friends have with the issue. If miracles had as their primary purpose authentication, then it would be expected that they should decline as those being authenticated were indeed accepted by the church as true representatives of God bearing His inspired message. Looking at the experience of Paul, since his life is most fully depicted in Acts and since his writings cover the full range of the period in question, the loss of ability came with the gain of acceptance and the spread of the gospel throughout the limits of the Roman Empire. By his Roman imprisonment, his apostleship was no longer questioned. This is reflected in the change in the tenor of his prison and post-prison epistles as compared to Galatians, Romans, and the Corinthians.

There are three major views concerning the purpose of miracles. The first two are held by non-Pentecostals. Miracles are seen first as either establishing the church or second as authenticating the messenger. The third view, primarily held by those holding to present-day miracles through miracle workers, is that they were given to the church to aid in spreading the gospel and showing mercy. These will be discussed below.

Establishment of the Church

The first non-Pentecostal view concerning miracles in the first-century church understands that they served the purpose of establishing the church. Forge states it by saying, "This special dispensation of the miraculous was expedient because of the establishment of the new order of the church, and also the writing of the whole New Testament."[332] Habershon sees miracles ending once the transition to the church age was complete.[333] Lockyer affirms this position by saying, "Apostolic miracles established the Church as a divine institution, and once firmly established was mainly left to ordinary providence."[334] This position has merit, and the New Testament's record of Paul's loss of miracle-working power supports this view. By his Roman imprisonment, the church was well established throughout the Roman world, and Paul had to look beyond its borders for new territories to claim. He wrote his hopes to the church in Rome and said:

> And thus I aspired to preach the gospel, not where Christ was already named, that I might not build upon another man's foundation; but as it is written, "They who had no news of Him shall see, and they who have not heard shall understand." For this reason I have often been hindered from coming to you; but now, with no further place for me in these regions, and since I have had for many years a longing to come to you whenever I go to Spain . . . [335]

However, the weakness of this position is its failure to account for Paul's references in 2 Corinthians 12:12 and Romans 15:18-19 to his miracles authenticating his apostleship. This leads to the second view.

---

332 Ibid., 20.
333 Habershon, Study of the Miracles, 245.
334 Lockyer, All the Miracles of the Bible, 19.
335 Rom 15:20-24.

APOSTOLIC *Signs and Gifts* OF THE SPIRIT

Authentication of the Messengers

Miracle authority was given to the apostolic generation to authenticate the men and their message.[336] This is the predominant view as well as the most supportable. Considering the revelation question, MacArthur linked tongues, healings, and miracles to the authentication of "an era of new revelation."[337] Based on Romans 15:18-19, 2 Corinthians 12:12, and Hebrews 2:4, Mayhue concludes, "God's primary purpose for miracles was to authenticate His messengers." He further argues that Paul, in the 2 Corinthians passage, "states emphatically that the marks (*semeia*) of an apostle were signs, wonders, and miracles."[338] Booth sees the record of Acts reflecting Paul's need to be recognized as a legitimate apostle in that Luke provided a record of Paul's miracles which paralleled Peter's.[339] Hillis sees the same relationship as true for those who were not apostles. He says, "Evidently the manifestation of healing power in Philip's ministry at Samaria was for the direct purpose of establishing the authority of the Gospel message and the church among the Samaritans."[340] Building from this relationship between miracles and their workers, Frost concludes that, "The apostolic miracles, therefore, were the divine sign to mankind that God had chosen the apostolic company as Christ's special representatives and messengers. It follows, for this reason that their miracles of healing are not necessarily to be repeated." He sees miracles remaining in a state of abatement for the rest of the church age and reappearing when God brings in the Kingdom program once again.[341]

This position is strengthened greatly by the evidence of Paul's

---

[336] Beals, "Significance of Miracles," 53-54; Forge, "The Doctrine of Miracles in the Apostolic Church," 10; Graber, "Temporary Gifts," 56; Howard C. Kee, *Miracles in the Early Christian World* (London: Yale University Press, 1983), 171.

[337] MacArthur, *The Charismatics*, 77.

[338] Richard L. Mayhue, *Divine Healing Today* (Chicago: Moody Press, 1983), 73.

[339] Booth, "The Purpose of Miracles," 188.

[340] Hillis, *Tongues, Healing, and You!* Second section, 22.

[341] Frost, *Miraculous Healing*, 127-29.

three friends' non-healings. Their location at the end of his ministry, after he was well established as the apostle to the Gentiles and within a time frame when Peter felt comfortable referring to his writings as Scripture (2 Pet 3:14-16), argues for his inability to heal to be the result of a lost need for authentication. Paul was unable to help them, even under distressing circumstances, which would have been greatly relieved by his intervention. Though miracles certainly served other functions, such as demonstrating mercy and establishing the church, their primary purpose was authenticating the message and the messenger. Once those messengers were accepted as sent from God, He no longer needed to authenticate them further.

Furtherance of the Gospel and Mercy

The third major view concerning the purpose of miracles, held principally by Pentecostals, is that they were performed in order to spread the gospel and show mercy.[342] Borgen says healing took a central place in Paul's ministry and that "Jesus was proclaimed as physician and healings were carried out in his name."[343] Wagner sees healing being an integral part of the gospel commission.[344] De Wet holds to their purpose being principally that of drawing "public attention to the power of God in order to open unsaved people's hearts to the message of the Gospel."[345] Though he does not hold to spreading the gospel as the primary purpose of miracles, Graber understands Paul's comment in Romans 15:18-19 as referring to his miracle-working power as an instrument "which Christ used for the furtherance of the Gospel among the Gentiles."[346]

---

342 Leo R. Van Dolson, "When the Doctor is Baffled," *Ministry* 53: 5 (May 1980): 20; John Sims, *Power with Purpose* (Cleveland: Pathway Press, 1984), 101-105.
343 Borgen, "Miracles of Healing in the New Testament," 92.
344 Wagner, *Church Growth and the Whole Gospel* (New York: Harper & Row, 1981), 15-17.
345 De Wet, "Biblical Basis of Signs and Wonders," 30.
346 Graber, "Temporary Gifts," 63.

There are strong arguments against this view. Hillis disagrees with this position and states his objection by saying that "neither He nor His disciples made healing their basic ministry. When they did heal, it was fundamentally a means to an end ... to establish His authority as the Son of God and to demonstrate His right to forgive sins."[347] Booth understands spreading the gospel and showing mercy to be only secondary, specialized purposes of the apostolic miracles.[348] Forge damages their position when he states, "The purpose of gospel miracles seems less effective to the Gentiles than to the Jews who had been schooled to accept them in their proper light, which was to authenticate the message and the messenger as from God."[349] This can be demonstrated especially from Paul's experiences at Lystra (Acts 14:8-18), in which the Gentiles tried to worship him, and on Malta (Acts 28:1-10), where his resistance to viper bites caused the people to think he was a god. Such a response never occurred within Jewish contexts. Interestingly, though he healed all who came to him on Malta, and though they honored him with many marks of respect, Luke did not report that faith resulted from those works of power.

The place of Paul's unhealed companions is damaging in the argument for miracles continuing due to their place in turning the hearts of men to respond to the proclamation of the gospel or in providing mercy. In the case of all three, it can be argued that their healings would have certainly demonstrated mercy upon each man. Also, though there may not have been any unbelievers present, the men would certainly serve better in the furtherance of the gospel in good health than while incapacitated. And, assuming there were unbelievers present (which is very probable with Paul's house arrest in Rome and his statement

---

347 Hillis, Tongues, Healing, and You!, 7.
348 Booth, "The Purpose of Miracles," 194.
349 Forge, "The Doctrine of Miracles in the Apostolic Church," 32.

in Philippians 1:12-13), their illnesses should have provided a prime opportunity to demonstrate God's power. Therefore, Paul's unhealed companions mitigate against both mercy and aiding as a principal purpose of miracles in the first century.

7

The Occurrence And Significance

Of Miracles Today

God Still Miraculously Intervenes

Whether one feels all miraculous gifts are in the past, only the "sign" gifts are in the past, or that all gifts continue to be manifested in the body of Christ, it is fair to say that everyone should agree that God still miraculously intervenes in our world today. To every saint, I would warn: Don't throw out God working in the world miraculously. Don't let our Western scientific worldview blind us to the acts of God around us that are clearly God's doing and not coincidences or something that can be explained away. We should not be the ones explaining away everything that appears supernatural. However, we also should not be gullible.

Scripture warns us that Satan can imitate God's power with false signs and wonders. He enables his servants, even human agents, to do the same. During the Day of the Lord, the Great Tribulation, Satan's main agents, the "beasts" out of the sea and earth (Rev 13), will deceive the whole world with their false signs and wonders. One may argue that they will involve trickery because they are called "false" by John. This is possible. However, "false" can also indicate the false claim that they are works of power from God and not Satan. Their falseness arises from their role in deception in the same way a false prophet could be one hundred percent accurate in his prophecies while leading people astray from obedience to God. Balaam was a false prophet because of his motives and actions to get Israel to sin against God, not his predictive success rate.

As God has acted throughout human history, He remains active in the world today. It is not solely in the convicting ministry of the Holy Spirit (John 16:8-11) that God works today. He continues to answer prayer and intervene according to His own will when and where He desires. The command and promise of Hebrews 13:1-2, that by showing hospitality, some believers have entertained angels, is not restricted to the first century either. To believe the frequency of miraculous interventions declined after the apostles passed from the scene does not mean one does not believe God is actively intervening through miracles today.

God Can Miraculously Intervene with Miracles Similar to Spiritual Gifts

When one accepts God's continuing intervention in the world, does this necessarily require the continuance of the "miraculous" spiritual gifts, sometimes called the "sign gifts"? It seems best to say that God's miraculous intervention can include things like speaking another language or healing someone. However, the person used by God might never be used in that manner again. This would mean that the person does not have the "gift" of tongues or healing per se but that God chose to meet a need at that time in that way. Further, God does not necessarily intervene in the same way everywhere but can base the nature of His interventions on the needs of that region. For example, there are many reports of Muslims having visions of Jesus. Visions are an integral part of Arab culture. So, could God use that to bring people to faith where there is no gospel voice at this time? The best answer is to say that the frequency of the reports may argue for God doing just that. At the same time, it would be less likely to find Him intervening in that same way in a culture that grants little or no significance to dreams. In those cultures characterized by demonic activity, where animism continues to be practiced, we should expect to see more supernatural interventions by God. But, again, what about in a Western culture where demonic activity is not as blatant? As a resident of the United States and educated in a secular university with a naturalistic scientific worldview, it would be easy to dismiss the reports of supernatural acts and reject them with scientific explanations. However, God's Word clearly stands in contrast to the naturalistic worldview prevalent in the United States. So, it seems good to share some of my own experiences that will illustrate how I see God intervening today in the culture around me.

Personal Observations

One Sunday, after I had announced to my church that I was resigning my commission in the Army to attend seminary, a lady in the church approached me. She explained to me that her daughter was experiencing serious health issues, including places in her legs "sinking." She asked me to pray for her daughter's healing. Instead of saying yes, I suddenly felt a compulsion to say something to her. I told her that I felt her daughter had a personal issue that needed to be resolved between her and God. When that was resolved, she would get better. The next week the lady sought me out in church and told me that she had shared what I said to her daughter. Her daughter admitted that she had been angry with God because He had made her so short that her feet could not reach the floor when she sat in a chair. Her symptoms disappeared as soon as she admitted that and "got things right" with God. Granted, one might argue that her "illness" may have been psychosomatic, and resolving things removed the mental cause. However, my insight had nothing to do with wisdom or knowledge of the girl. It came "out of the air," in a sense. I would see it as an insight God granted me to meet that lady and her daughter's needs.

Soon after I had left the Army to attend seminary, I had a conversation in my brother's home with some friends of his (husband and wife) who had dropped in to visit. As we were talking about various things, like politics and weather, we turned to moral issues. I felt this need to bring up a specific sin issue at that point. My brother's friends listened to what I said and left soon afterward. After his friends left, my brother told me that the couple was struggling with that sin. Was this the gift, sometimes called "a word of knowledge"? Was it a prophetic gift? I have neither spiritual gift. It only happened these two times without my seeking or expecting it. I cannot make it happen. I don't have the gift.

When I was a young boy, my father told of a situation once in a church where the pastor had begun the introduction to his sermon and suddenly paused, thought a second or two, and announced that he felt God was leading him to speak on a different issue. He changed the passage and preached about a particular sin. After the service, a man walked up to him and told him it was his sin. He knew the pastor did not know him (a first-time visitor), and the pastor changed his subject just as the man walked in. One can conclude that God impressed the pastor to change his message specifically because He was at work in the life of the man who needed to repent.

Stories can be told throughout the evangelical world of people praying for sick family, friends, or church members and seeing God miraculously heal them. By miraculous, I mean that doctors could not explain the sudden healing which did not result from medication or surgery. As a child growing up in deep south Southern Baptist churches, I remember routinely hearing prayers requesting God to heal people miraculously. I have prayed them myself and anticipated an answer. I have not seen that as often in Baptist churches in recent years. It seems the Baptist world asks less often. It should not be such. Today we see more instances of God's miraculous intervention within the Pentecostal/Charismatic world because their theology leads them to ask in faith. They experience more miraculous answers to prayer because they ask more often. James' words should be heeded here, "You have not because you ask not" (Jas 4:3). Granted, the context of his words does not have to do with healing. However, the principle still stands. God waits for us to ask before He intervenes. If we would ask more, we would see Him miraculously intervene more. But, even in asking, how can we be certain it is from God?

Can We Discern Between Real and False Miracles?

What makes a miracle real? Is it in the eyes of the beholder, or are there standards we can apply to discern between real and false miracles? These questions point us toward the problem we face today: the presence of false miracle workers claiming to be faith healers and giving reports of miraculous healings, often unverifiable. Yet, real miracles can and do occur. God does intervene today. And we should be discerning in order to recognize true miracles while rejecting the false. Why? God is not glorified by fake miracles. God is only glorified by what is true. To call a non-miracle a miracle does not bring Him glory but attributes something that is not true to Him. So, we need to know that it is a miracle before we attribute the event to God's intervention.

As noted at the beginning of this study, miracles, by their nature, cannot be repeated through human agency. The exception would be someone given healing authority by God, a miracle worker. However, anyone claiming this authority should be able to exercise it at will and be medically verifiable. As said earlier, these divine interventions should have the fingerprints of God on them, just as Jesus' miracles did. They should fit the patterns of Jesus, the apostles, and others of their generation. We should beware of psychosomatic illnesses and their tendency to respond to suggestion. That is not a miracle but a natural human reaction. Partial healing, slow healing, or temporary healings are not miracles. We need to recognize this and be discerning. If we practice discernment and pray for God to act, we will see His answers to our prayers and be able to glorify Him as a result truly.

8

Conclusion

Where should we stand on the issue of miracles and miracle workers today? It seems best to say that the debate between proponents of the modern healing movement and those holding to a cessation of miracles in the first century hinges upon the question of any decline.[350] The Bennetts, arguing the Charismatic position, say, "Paul's power in the Holy Spirit did not decrease as he grew older. We find him manifesting God's miraculous keeping and healing power more strongly, if anything, in the last chapter of Acts, than in the earlier times (Acts 27–28). Paul never slowed down even in his old age."[351] However, Acts 28 was not the end of Paul's ministry or of church history.

The evidence examined, especially concerning the men whom Paul was unable to heal, argues for a decline in his ability to perform miracles near the end of his ministry, not a continuance. This decline is noticeable, not within the record of Acts, but within the record of those epistles written following the inception of Paul's first Roman imprisonment. Their silence is united with Paul's own testimony of being unable to help Epaphroditus, having to leave behind Trophimus, and only offering Timothy medical counsel to point toward a loss of ability. Alone, the si-

---
350 Hummel, "Healing: Our Double Standard?," 28.
351 Dennis and Rita Bennett, *The Holy Spirit and You* (Plainfield: Logos International, 1971), 131.

lence of the various epistles would not be conclusive. Combined with the other evidence, their silence becomes evidential. Paul was unable to perform the same miracles he had at the beginning of his ministry at its end.[352] Further, this would then be expected to be the experience of the church as a whole in his day. Ryrie reflects this understanding when he says, "The important thing here is to understand that even those who lived just prior to A.D. 70, before the close of the canon of Scripture, did not see and did not have some of the signs and wonders and miracles that the contemporaries of Christ had experienced."[353] Thus the evidence of Scripture weighs favorably toward the view that miracles declined as their usefulness in God's purpose ended.

Opposing the theological arguments from the texts of Scripture, such as Hebrews 2, is the more pragmatic approach of the proponents of modern faith healing. Oral Roberts, made famous for his claims of miraculous gifts, argues for modern miracles experientially. He says, "The fact is, my friend, you can spend hours, days, even weeks in arguing whether or not miracles still happen today and get nowhere. If you really want to know, find someone who has experienced a miracle. Ask them what they think! Or better still, ask God to give you a miracle. Once you, or someone close to you, has experienced a miracle, there will be no question in your mind."[354] In contrast to such an argument is the response of Edgar:

> Proponents of the charismatic movement have managed to shift the burden of proof regarding the temporary nature of some gifts to their opponents. They have done this by assuming that all things are to be the same throughout

---

[352] Booth, "The Purpose of Miracles," 202-203; Knuteson, "Are You Waiting for a Miracle?," 22; Brian G. Peterson, "The Significance of Miracles within the Transitional Framework of the Book of Acts" (ThM thesis, DTS, 1976), 30; Whitcomb, "Does God Want Christians to Perform Miracles Today?," 7.

[353] Ryrie, "Greater Works than These," 33.

[354] Roberts, A Daily Guide to Miracles, 185.

the church age, and they have demanded proof otherwise. ... Since the facts of church history reveal that the Holy Spirit has not been functioning in all the ways that He did in the book of Acts, then the basic assumption that all things remain the same is false. It is contrary to the facts; therefore the burden of proof properly falls upon those who claim that all gifts are for the entire duration of the church age.[355]

As seen in this book, there seems to be good evidence within the New Testament that modern proponents of faith healing need addressing before they can claim that God *must* work the same today as He did at the beginning of the church. Even within the time frame of the New Testament writers, there are at least strong indicators that all did not remain the same in respect to the manner God was choosing to work in and through them. However, that does not stop God from acting today in and through individuals in response to the prayers of His people or the good pleasure of His will.

As discussed in previous chapters, the problem with either approach, though still popular today among many, is the need to clearly define and recognize what is truly miraculous. Crying out, "It's a miracle!" does not make it so. However, it is just as wrong to ignore or deny the miraculous act of God when it occurs. Yet, one question, I am convinced, can be answered.

There are no miracle workers today. No one has the apostolic authority experienced by the early church in which individuals minister who has the ability to heal at will. Paul did. Peter did. The other apostles did, as did others in the early church. However, there is a more important issue, that of unity within the body of Christ.

---

[355] Edgar, Miraculous Gifts: Are They for Today?,267.

APOSTOLIC *Signs and Gifts* OF THE SPIRIT

When Jesus prayed His high priestly prayer in John 17, He prayed primarily for unity within the church. The nature of this unity was defined earlier by Him as love for one another (John 13:34-35). This mutual love convinces the world that we are Jesus' disciples, not the signs on our churches or the Bibles we carry. Jesus knew back then that there would be theological differences between churches and denominations, even groups within churches. Yet He prayed for unity. This unity does not come through theological compromise to achieve absolute agreement but through a commitment to one another as brothers and sisters in Christ. We all experience the privilege of being members of the household of God (Eph 2:19), and we are expected to act like it. What does this mean to those of us who are serious about our faith and desire to be faithful to our Lord?

Our challenge is to be accepting and understanding toward our fellow saints, even when we disagree with them. The cessationist camp needs to restrict its diatribe and divisive language. It also needs to ask God more often to intervene and not be blind to His action when He does. Look for His hand in the world around us, especially within the lives of His people. At the same time, the Pentecostal world needs to be discerning between what is miraculous and what is not. Don't stop asking God to act. But also discern between the false claims of some who call miraculous that which is not. And for both groups, there is a better way.

Paul pointed us to the role of love in controlling the misuse of spiritual gifts in 1 Corinthians 13. We need to practice that as well. Further, in most of his epistles, we can see the pattern with Paul of emphasizing three things every believer should pursue: faith, hope, and love (1 Cor 13:13). We should never pursue gifts that will draw attention to us. God will give us what the church needs, not what the individual wants. When we pursue faith, hope, and love, we will express God's love for individuals and achieve the work of God rather than magnifying people. We can be friends and disagree. Remember, we live in a world that is hostile to both groups. Let's not lock horns but lock arms. This is what we were chosen by God to do. This is how we glorify Him. This is more important than winning the argument.

BIBLIOGRAPHY

Books

Abbott, T. K. *A Critical and Exegetical Commentary on the Epistles to the Ephesians and to the Colossians.* The International Critical Commentary. Edinburgh: T. & T. Clark, n.d.

Allen, David L. *Hebrews.* The New American Commentary. Nashville: B & H Publishing Group, 2010.

Anderson, Robert. *The Silence of God.* New York: Dodd Mead & Company, 1897.

Baker, C. F. *A Dispensational Theology.* Grand Rapids: Grace Bible College Publications, 1971.

Barbieri, Louis A., Jr. *First and Second Peter.* Everyman's Bible Commentary. Chicago: Moody Press, 1975.

—. "Matthew." In *The Bible Knowledge Commentary: An Exposition of the Scriptures.* Edited by J. F. Walvoord and R. B. Zuck. Volume 2. Wheaton, IL: Victor Books, 1985.

Barclay, William. *The Letters to Timothy, Titus, and Philemon.* Revised edition. Philadelphia: The Westminster Press, 1975.

Barrett, C. K. *The First Epistle to the Corinthians.* Black's New Testament Commentary. London: Continuum, 1968.

—. *The Signs of an Apostle.* Philadelphia: Fortress Press, 1972.

Beare, F. W. *A Commentary on the Epistle to the Philippians.* Second edition. London: Adam & Charles Black, 1969.

Beasley-Murray, George R. *John.* Word Biblical Commentary. Vol. 36. Dallas: Word, Inc., 2002.

Bennett, Dennis and Rita. *The Holy Spirit and You.* Plainfield: Logos International, 1971.

Betz, Hans Dieter. *Galatians.* Hermeneia—A Critical and Historical Commentary on the Bible. Philadelphia: Fortress Press, 1979.

Blomberg, Craig. *Matthew.* The New American Commentary. Vol. 22. Nashville: Broadman & Holman Publishers, 1992.

Blue, J. Ronald. "James." In *The Bible Knowledge Commentary: An Exposition of the Scriptures.* Eds. J. F. Walvoord and R. B. Zuck. Vol. 2. Wheaton, IL: Victor Books, 1985.

Blue, Ken. *Authority to Heal.* Downers Grove, IL: InterVarsity Press, 1987.

Blum, Edwin A. "John" In *The Bible Knowledge Commentary: An Exposition of the Scriptures.* Eds. J. F. Walvoord and R. B. Zuck. Vol. 2. Wheaton, IL: Victor Books, 1985.

Bock, Darrell L. *Luke: 1:1–9:50*. Baker Exegetical Commentary on the New Testament. Vol. 1. Grand Rapids, MI: Baker Academic, 1994.

Borchert, Gerald L. *John 1–11*. The New American Commentary. Vol. 25A. Nashville: Broadman & Holman Publishers, 1996.

Bresden, Herald, with James F. Scheer. *Need a Miracle?* Old Tappan: Fleming H. Revell Company, 1979.

Brooks, James A. *Mark*. The New American Commentary. Vol 23. Nashville: Broadman & Holman Publishers, 1991.

Brown, Colin. *Miracles and the Critical Mind*. Grand Rapids: William B. Eerdmans, 1984.

Brown, Colin. *That You May Believe*. Grand Rapids: William B. Eerdmans, 1985.

Bruce, F. F. *Paul: Apostle of the Heart Set Free*. Grand Rapids: William B. Eerdmans, 1977.

—. *The Book of Acts*. The New International Commentary on the New Testament. Grand Rapids: William B. Eerdmans, n.d.

—. *The Epistles of John*. Grand Rapids: William B. Eerdmans, 1970.

—. *1 and 2 Thessalonians*. Word Bible Commentary. Waco: Word Books, 1982.

Bruner, Frederick D. *A Theology of the Holy Spirit*. Grand Rapids: William B. Eerdmans, 1970.

Burns, R. M. *The Great Debate on Miracles*. Lewisburg: Bucknell University Press, 1981.

Carson, D. A. *The Gospel according to John*. The Pillar New Testament Commentary. Grand Rapids: William B. Eerdmans, 1991.

Chantry, Walter G. *Signs of the Apostles*. Carlisle: The Banner of Truth Trust, 1973.

Collange, Jean-Francois. *The Epistle of Saint Paul to the Philippians*. Translated by A. W. Heathcote. London: Epworth Press, 1979.

Copeland, Kenneth. *Walking in the Realm of the Miraculous*. Fort Worth: KCP Publications, 1979.

Craddock, Fred B. "Philippians." In *Interpretation*. Atlanta: John Knox Press, 1985.

Dalton, Robert C. *Tongues Like As of Fire*. Springfield: The Gospel Publishing House, 1945.

Davids, Peter H. *The Epistle of James: A Commentary on the Greek Text*. The New International Greek Testament Commentary. Grand Rapids: William B. Eerdmans, 1982.

De Groot, A. *The Bible on Miracles*. Translated by Jos A. Roessen. De Pere: St. Norbert Abbey Press, 1966.

Dodd, Thomas J. *Miracles: Were They, or Were They Not, Performed by Jesus? A Question of Fact, Not Science or Theology.* New York: Eaton & Mains. Copyright 1899 by the Western Methodist Book Concern.

Duffield, Guy P. and Nathaniel M. Van Cleave. *Foundations of Pentecostal Theology.* Los Angeles: L. I. F. E. Bible College, 1983.

Edgar, Thomas R. *Miraculous Gifts: Are They for Today?* Neptune: Loizeaux Brothers, 1983.

Edwards, James R. *The Gospel according to Mark.* The Pillar New Testament Commentary. Grand Rapids, MI: Eerdmans, 2002.

Ellingworth, Paul and Eugene Albert Nida. *A Handbook on the Letter to the Hebrews.* UBS Handbook Series. New York: United Bible Societies, 1994.

Flynn, Leslie B. *19 Gifts of the Spirit.* Wheaton, IL: Victor Books, 1994.

Foster, Lewis. *John: Unlocking the Scriptures for You.* Standard Bible Studies. Cincinnati, OH: Standard, 1987.

Frame, James E. *A Critical and Exegetical Commentary on the Epistles of St. Paul to the Thessalonians.* The International Critical Commentary. Edinburgh: T. & T. Clark, 1912.

Fridrichsen, Anton. *The Problem of Miracle in Primitive Christianity.* Translated by Roy A. Harrisville and John S. Hanson. Minneapolis: Augsburg Publishing House, 1972.

Frost, Henry W. *Miraculous Healing.* New York: Fleming H. Revell Company, 1931–1939.

Fuller, Reginald H. *Interpreting the Miracles.* London: SCM Press LTD, 1963.

Gaebelein, A. C. *The Acts of the Apostles.* New York: Publication Office "Our Hope," n.d.

Gaffin, Richard B., Jr. "A Cessationist View." In *Are Miraculous Gifts for Today? 4 Views,* ed. Wayne A. Grudem. Counterpoints. Grand Rapids: Zondervan Publishing House, 1966.

Gangel, Kenneth O. *John.* Holman New Testament Commentary. Vol. 4. Nashville: Broadman & Holman Publishers, 2000.

Garland, David E. *1 Corinthians.* Baker Exegetical Commentary on the New Testament. Grand Rapids: Baker Academic, 2003.

Geisler, Norman. *Signs and Wonders.* Wheaton: Tyndale House Publishers, 1988.

Gordon, A. J. *The Ministry of Healing.* New York: Fleming H. Revell Company, 1882.

Gordon, Ernest. *The Fact of Miracle.* Francestown: Marshall Jones Company, 1955.

Gordon, George A. *Religion and Miracle.* New York: Houghton Mifflin Company, 1909.

Gromacki, Robert G. *Stand True to the Charge.* Grand Rapids: Baker Book House, 1982.

Grudem, Wayne. *Systematic Theology.* 2nd ed. Grand Rapids: Zondervan Academic, 2020.

Guelich, Robert A. *Mark 1–8:26.* Word Biblical Commentary. Vol. 34A. Dallas: Word, Inc., 1998.

Guthrie, Donald. "John" In *New Bible Commentary: 21st Century Edition,* edited by D. A. Carson *et al.*, 4th ed. Downers Grove: Inter-Varsity Press, 1994.

—. *New Testament Introduction.* Downers Grove: InterVarsity Press, 1970.

Habershon, Ada R. *The Study of the Miracles.* London: Pickering & Englis, n.d.

Hagner, Donald A. *Matthew 1–13.* Word Biblical Commentary. Vol. 33A. Dallas: Word, Inc., 1998.

Hendriksen, William and Simon J. Kistemaker. *Exposition of the Gospel According to Matthew.* Volume 9. New Testament Commentary. Grand Rapids: Baker Book House, 1953–2001.

Henry, Carl F. H. *God, Revelation, and Authority.* Volume 6. Wheaton, IL: Crossway Books, 1999.

Heron, Alasdair I. C. *The Holy Spirit.* Philadelphia: The Westminster Press, 1983.

Hiebert, D. Edmond. *Second Timothy.* Chicago: Moody Press, 1958.

Hillis, Don W. *Tongues, Healing, and You!* Grand Rapids: Baker Book House, 1969.

Hughes, Philip E. *The Second Epistle to the Corinthians.* The New International Commentary on the New Testament. Grand Rapids: William B. Eerdmans, 1962.

Hughes, Robert B. and J. Carl Laney. *Tyndale Concise Bible Commentary.* The Tyndale Reference Library. Wheaton, IL: Tyndale House Publishers, 2001.

Hume, David. *Of Miracles.* La Salle: Open Court, 1985. (written by Hume in 1748).

Hunt, Dwight L. "The First Epistle of Paul the Apostle to the Corinthians." In *The Grace New Testament Commentary,* edited by Robert N. Wilkin. Denton, TX: Grace Evangelical Society, 2010.

Jackson, Edgar N. *The Role of Faith in the Process of Healing.* Minneapolis: Winston Press, 1981.

Jamieson, Robert, A. R. Fausset, and David Brown. *Commentary Critical and Explanatory on the Whole Bible.* Vol. 2. Oak Harbor, WA: Logos Research Systems, Inc., 1997.

Jorstad, Erling. Editor. *The Holy Spirit in Today's Church.* Nashville: Abingdon Press, 1973.

Kee, Howard Clark. *Miracle in the Early Christian World.* London: Yale University Press, 1983.

Keener, Craig S. *Miracles: The Credibility of the New Testament Accounts*. Vols. 1 & 2. Grand Rapids: Baker, 2011.

Keller, Ernst and Marie-Luise. *Miracles in Dispute*. Translated by Margaret Kohl. Chapter 5 was written especially for the English edition. SCM Press, 1969.

Kistemaker, Simon J. and William Hendriksen. *Exposition of the First Epistle to the Corinthians*. Volume 18. New Testament Commentary. Grand Rapids: Baker Book House, 1953–2001.

—. *Exposition of Hebrews*. New Testament Commentary. Vol. 15. Grand Rapids: Baker Book House, 1953–2001.

—. *Exposition of James and the Epistles of John*. New Testament Commentary. Vol. 14. Grand Rapids: Baker Book House, 1953–2001.

Koenig, John. *Charismata: God's Gifts for God's People*. Philadelphia: The Westminster Press, 1978.

Köstenberger, Andreas J. *John*. Baker Exegetical Commentary on the New Testament. Grand Rapids: Baker Academic, 2004.

Kydd, Ronald A. N. *Charismatic Gifts in the Early Church*. Peabody, MA: Hendrickson Publishers, 1984.

Lane, William L. *Hebrews 1–8*. Word Biblical Commentary. Vol. 47A. Dallas: Word, Inc., 1998.

Lange, John Peter and Philip Schaff. *A Commentary on the Holy Scriptures: Matthew*. Bellingham, WA: Logos Bible Software, 2008.

Lawton, John Stewart. *Miracles and Revelation*. New York: Association Press, n.d.

Lea, Thomas D. *Hebrews, James*. Holman New Testament Commentary. Vol. 10. Nashville: Broadman & Holman, 1999.

Lenski, R. C. H. *The Interpretation of St. Matthew's Gospel*. Minneapolis: Augsburg Publishing House, 1961.

—. *The Interpretation of St. Mark's Gospel*. Minneapolis: Augsburg Publishing House, 1961.

—. *The Interpretation of St. Paul's Epistles to the Galatians, to the Ephesians, and to the Philippians*. Minneapolis: Augsburg Publishing House, 1961.

—. *The Interpretation of St. Paul's First and Second Epistles to the Corinthians*. Minneapolis: Augsburg Publishing House, 1963.

—. *The Interpretation of the Epistle to the Hebrews and of the Epistle of James*. Columbus, OH: Lutheran Book Concern, 1938.

Lightfoot, J. B. *St. Paul's Epistle to the Philippians*. London: Macmillan & Company, 1913; reprint edition. Grand Rapids: Zondervan, 1953.

Lincoln, Andrew T. *The Gospel according to Saint John*. Black's New Testament Commentary. London: Continuum, 2005.

Lockyer, Herbert. *All the Men of the Bible*. Grand Rapids: Zondervan, 1958.

—. *All the Miracles of the Bible*. Grand Rapids: Zondervan, 1961.

Longenecker, Richard N. "The Acts of the Apostles." In *The Expositor's Bible Commentary*. 9:207-573, Grand Rapids: Zondervan, 1981.

Lowery, David K. "1 Corinthians" In *The Bible Knowledge Commentary: An Exposition of the Scriptures*, edited by J. F. Walvoord and R. B. Zuck. Volume 2. Wheaton, IL: Victor Books, 1985.

MacArthur, John F., Jr. *1 Corinthians*. Chicago: Moody Press, 1984.

—. *Charismatic Chaos*. Grand Rapids: Zondervan, 1992.

—. *The Charismatics*. Grand Rapids: Zondervan, 1978.

MacDonald, William. *Believer's Bible Commentary: Old and New Testaments*, edited by Arthur Farstad. Nashville: Thomas Nelson, 1995.

Marshall, I. Howard. *1 and 2 Thessalonians*. New Century Bible Commentary. Grand Rapids: William B. Eerdmans, 1983.

—. *The Epistles of John*. New International Commentary on the New Testament. Grand Rapids: William B. Eerdmans, 1978.

—. *The Gospel of Luke: A Commentary on the Greek Text*. New International Greek Testament Commentary. Exeter: Paternoster Press, 1978.

Martin, Ralph P. *James*. Word Biblical Commentary. Vol. 48. Dallas: Word, Inc., 1998.

—. *Philippians*. New Century Bible Commentary. Grand Rapids: William B. Eerdmans, 1976.

Mayhue, Richard L. *Divine Healing Today*. Chicago: Moody Press, 1983.

McCrossan, T. J. *Bodily Healing and the Atonement*. Seattle: T. J. McCrossan Publisher, 1930.

McReynolds, Paul R. *Mark: Unlocking the Scriptures for You*. Standard Bible Studies. Cincinnati, OH: Standard, 1989.

Miller, Wayman D. *Modern Divine Healing*. Fort Worth: Miller Publishing Co., 1956.

Moo, Douglas J. *The Letter of James*. The Pillar New Testament Commentary. Grand Rapids: Eerdmans, 2000.

Morris, Leon. "Hebrews." In *The Expositor's Bible Commentary*. Vol.12:3-158. Grand Rapids: Zondervan, 1981.

—. *The Gospel according to Matthew*. The Pillar New Testament Commentary. Grand Rapids: W.B. Eerdmans, 1992.

Motyer, J. A. *The Message of Philippians: Jesus our Joy*. Downers Grove: InterVarsity Press, 1984.

Moule, Handley C. G. *Philippian Studies*. London: Pickering & Inglis, n.d.

Mounce, William D. *Basics of Biblical Greek*. 3rd ed. Grand Rapids: Zondervan, 2009.

Murray, John. *The Epistle to the Romans*. Grand Rapids: William B. Eerdmans, 1965, one volume edition published in September 1968.

Neal, Emily G. *The Healing Power of Christ.* New York: Hawthorn Books, 1972.

Neil, William. *The Epistle of Paul to the Thessalonians.* The Moffatt New Testament Commentary. New York: Harper, 1950.

Nolland, John. "Preface." In *The Gospel of Matthew: A Commentary on the Greek Text.* New International Greek Testament Commentary. Grand Rapids: William B. Eerdmans, 2005.

Paterson, Andrew. *Opening Up John's Gospel.* Opening Up Commentary. Leominster: Day One Publications, 2010.

Pfeiffer, Charles F. and Everett Falconer Harrison, eds., *The Wycliffe Bible Commentary: New Testament.* Chicago: Moody Press, 1962.

Pratt, Richard L. Jr. *I & II Corinthians.* Holman New Testament Commentary. Vol. 7. Nashville: Broadman & Holman Publishers, 2000.

Rainy, Robert. *The Epistle to the Philippians.* The Expositor's Bible. Edited by W. Robertson Nicoll. New York: Hodder & Stoughton, n.d.

Ramsay, W. M. *The Teaching of Paul in Terms of the Present Day.* London: Hodder and Stoughton, 1913.

Redford, Doug. *The New Testament Church: Acts-Revelation.* Standard Reference Library: New Testament. Vol. 2. Cincinnati, OH: Standard Pub., 2007.

Richardson, Kurt A. *James.* The New American Commentary. Vol. 36. Nashville: Broadman & Holman Publishers, 1997.

Ridderbos, Herman N. *The Epistle of Paul to the Churches of Galatia.* Grand Rapids: William B. Eerdmans, 1953.

Roberts, Oral. *A Daily Guide to Miracles.* Old Tappan: Fleming H. Revell Company, 1975.

—. *Exactly How You May Receive Your Healing Through Faith?* Tulsa, OK: Oral Roberts, 1958.

Robertson, A. T. *A Grammar of the Greek New Testament in the Light of Historical Research.* Nashville: Broadman Press, 1934.

—. *Word Pictures in the New Testament.* Nashville: Broadman Press, 1933.

Robertson, Pat. *My Prayer for You.* Old Tappan: Fleming H. Revell Company, 1977.

Ryrie, Charles C. *First and Second Thessalonians.* Everyman's Bible Commentary. Chicago: Moody Press, 1959.

—. *The Holy Spirit.* Chicago: Moody Press, 1965.

Schenck, Kenneth. *1 & 2 Corinthians: A Commentary for Bible Students.* Indianapolis, IN: Wesleyan Publishing House, 2006.

Sims, John. *Power with Purpose.* Cleveland: Pathway Press, 1984.

Staton, Knofel. *First Corinthians: Unlocking the Scriptures for You.* Standard Bible Studies. Cincinnati, OH: Standard, 1987.

Stott, John R. W. *Guard the Gospel.* Downers Grove: InterVarsity Press, 1973.

Sumrall, Ken. "Miracles and Healing." In *The Holy Spirit in Today's Church*, edited by Erling Jorstad. Nashville: Abingdon Press, 1973.

Talbert, Charles H. *Reading Corinthians: A Literary and Theological Commentary on 1 & 2 Corinthians*. Rev. ed. Reading the New Testament Series. Macon, GA: Smyth & Helwys Publishing, 2002.

Tenney, Merrill C. *John*. The Expositor's Bible Commentary. Vol. 9. Grand Rapids: Zondervan, 1981.

Thiessen, Henry C. *Introduction to the New Testament*. Grand Rapids: William B. Eerdmans, 1952.

Thiselton, Anthony C. *The First Epistle to the Corinthians: A Commentary on the Greek Text*. New International Greek Testament Commentary. Grand Rapids: William B. Eerdmans, 2000.

Thomas, Robert L. *Understanding Spiritual Gifts: A Verse-by-Verse Study of 1 Corinthians 12-14*. Revised. Grand Rapids: Kregel, 1999.

Thompson, J. M. *Miracles in the New Testament*. London: Edward Arnold, 1911.

Trail, Ronald. *An Exegetical Summary of 1 Corinthians 10–16*. 2nd ed. Dallas, TX: SIL International, 2008.

Trench, Richard C. *Notes on the Miracles of Our Lord*. New York: Fleming H. Revell Company, n.d.

—. *Synonyms of the New Testament*. 9th ed. Reprint. Grand Rapids: William B. Eerdmans, 1950.

Twelftree, Graham H. *Paul and the Miraculous: A Historical Reconstruction*. Grand Rapids: Baker Academic, 2013.

Utley, Robert J. *The Superiority of the New Covenant: Hebrews*. Study Guide Commentary Series. Vol. 10. Marshall, Texas: Bible Lessons International, 1999.

Varner, William. *James*. Evangelical Exegetical Commentary. Bellingham, WA: Lexham Press, 2012.

Vine, W. E. *The Epistles to Timothy and Titus*. Grand Rapids: Zondervan Publishing House, 1965.

Von Gerdtell, Ludwig. *Burning Questions of the Day. No. 2, "Have we Satisfactory Evidence of the New Testament Miracles?* Translated by Samuel H. Wilkinson. Revised by E. K. Simpson. London: John Bale, Sons & Danielsson, Ltd, 1907.

Wagner, C. Peter. *Church Growth and the Whole Gospel*. New York: Harper & Row, 1981.

—. *Look Out! The Pentecostals are Coming*. Carol Stream: Creation House, 1973.

—. *On the Crest of the Wave*. Ventura: Regal Books, 1983.

Walvoord, John F. *Philippians: Triumph in Christ*. Everyman's Bible Commentary. Chicago: Moody Press, 1971.

—. . *The Doctrine of the Holy Spirit*. Dallas: Dallas Theological Seminary, 1943.

—. *The Holy Spirit at Work Today.* Chicago: Moody Press, 1973.

Warfield, Benjamin B. *Counterfeit Miracles.* New York: Charles Scribner's Sons, 1918.

Weber, Stuart K. *Matthew.* Holman New Testament Commentary. Vol. 1. Nashville: Broadman & Holman Publishers, 2000.

Weldon, John, and Zola Levitt. *Psychic Healing.* Chicago: Moody Press, 1982.

Wessel, Walter W. *Mark.* The Expositor's Bible Commentary. Grand Rapids: Zondervan, 1984.

Westcott, B. F. ed. *The Epistle to the Hebrews the Greek Text with Notes and Essays.* 3rd ed. Classic Commentaries on the Greek New Testament. London: Macmillan, 1903.

Wilkinson, John. *Health and Healing.* The Handel Press, 1980.

Williams, J. Rodman. *The Gift of the Holy Spirit Today.* Plainfield: Logos International, 1980.

Wimber, John. *Power Evangelism.* San Francisco: Harper and Row, 1986.

—. *Power Healing.* San Francisco: Harper and Row, 1987.

Woychuk, N. A. *Exposition of Second Timothy.* St. Louis: Miracle Press, 1973.

Dictionaries, Encyclopedias, and Periodicals

Arndt, William, Frederick W. Danker, and Walter Bauer. *A Greek-English Lexicon of the New Testament and Other Early Christian Literature.* Chicago: University of Chicago Press, 2000.

Ball, Karen. "An Evaluation by Theologians." *Christian Life* (October 1982): 64-69.

Barry, John D. gen. ed. *Faithlife Study Bible.* Bellingham, WA: Lexham Press, 2016.

Bennet, Dennis. "Does God Want to Heal Everybody?" *Charisma* (September 1983): 56, 59-61.

Bishop, Joseph. "Jesus' Healing Presence." *Christian Life* (September 1983): 36-38.

Borgen, Peder. "Miracles of Healing in the New Testament" *Studia Theologica* 35 (1981): 91-106.

Braden, Charles S. "Study of Spiritual Healing in the Churches." *Pastoral Psychology* 5 (May 1954): 9-15.

Bradley, Michael. "Having Faith and Belief That God Can Actually Heal You." www.bible-knowledge.com/faith-god-can-heal-you (accessed November 29, 2018).

Bryan, William F. "Miraculous Continuity." *The Alliance Witness* (January 24, 1979): 3-4.

Carlston, Charles E. "The Question of Miracles." *Andover Newton Quarterly* 12 (November 1971): 99-107.

Cavnar, Nick. "Miracles: Do They Really Happen?" *New Covenant* (November 1982): 4-7.

Chesterton, G. K. "Miracles and Modern Civilization." *The Chesterton Review* 9 (August 1983): 197-201.

Clark, David. "Miracles Lead to Revivals." *Christian Life* (November 1982): 34-35.

Clement of Rome. "The First Epistle of Clement to the Corinthians." In *The Apostolic Fathers with Justin Martyr and Irenaeus*, edited by Alexander Roberts, James Donaldson, and A. Cleveland Coxe, Volume 1. The Ante-Nicene Fathers. Buffalo, NY: Christian Literature Company, 1885.

Compton, R. Bruce. "1 Corinthians 13:8–13 and the Cessation of Miraculous Gifts." *Detroit Baptist Seminary Journal* 9 (2004): 97-144.

Copeland, Gloria. "Take Your Healing—By Faith." www.hopefaithprayer.com/take-healing-faith-gloria-copeland (accessed November 29, 2018).

De Wet, Christiaan. "Biblical Basis of Signs and Wonders." *Christian Life* (October 1982): 28-34.

Dorpat, David. "Why Doesn't God Heal Everyone?" *New Covenant* (June 1980): 4-6.

Edgar, Thomas R. "Does God Heal the Body?" *Good News Broadcaster* (March 1981): 23-25.

The Eerdmans Bible Dictionary. Grand Rapids: William B. Eerdmans, 1987.

Enke, Dorothy. ". . . And Miracles Occur." *The Sunday School Times and Gospel Herald* (December 1, 1976): 8-9.

Evangelical Dictionary of Theology. 1984 edition. s.v. "Heal, Healing." by P. G. Chappell, 497-98; "Miracles." by J. D. Spiceland, 723-24; "Spiritual Gifts." by J. G. S. S. Thompson and W. A. Elwell, 1042-1046. Foubister, D. Ron. "Healing in the Liturgy of the Post-Apostolic Church." *Studia Biblica et Theologia* 9 (October 1979): 141-55.

Free Inquiry 6:3 (Summer 1986).

Funk, Robert W. "The Form of the New Testament Healing Miracle Story." *Semeia* 12 (1978): 57-95.

Geisler, Norman L. *Baker Encyclopedia of Christian Apologetics*. Grand Rapids: Baker Books 1999.

Greenwood, Marcia. "Faith and Healing." www.tgm.org/faithmp.htm (accessed November 29, 2018).

Grover, Paul. "Miracles: God-acts in History." *Interchange* 34 (1983): 35-40.

Hagin, Kenneth E. "Faith Brings Results." www.rhema.org/index.php?option =comcontent&view=article &id=1026:faith-brings-esults&-catid=46&Itemid=141 (accessed November 29, 2018).

Hamblin, Robert L. "Miracles in the Book of Acts." *Southwestern Journal of Theology* 17: 1 (Fall 1974): 19-34.

Houghton, Myron J. "A Reexamination of 1 Corinthians 13:8–13." *Bibliotheca Sacra* 153 (1996): 344-56.

Hubbard, David A. "Hazarding the Risks." *Christian Life* (October 1982): 36-38.

Hulse, Errol. "Can We do Miracles Today?" *The Banner of Truth* (July 1981): 21-28.

Hummel, Charles. "Healing: Our Double Standard?" *Christian Life* (November 1982): 27-28, 33.

Irvin, Maurice R. "He Hath Borne Our Pains." *The Alliance Witness* (November 22, 1972): 3-4.

Johnson, Ricky L. "Bar-Kochba." *Holman Illustrated Bible Dictionary*, edited by Chad Brand, Charles Draper, and Archie England (Nashville: Holman Bible Publishers, 2003), 171.

Keefauver, Larry. "Is Your Healing Contingent on Your Faith?" *Charisma Magazine* (10 a.m. EST, December 4, 2012). www.charismamag.com/spirit/supernatural/4537-the-myths-of-faith-healing (accessed November 29, 2018).

Knuteson, Roy E. "Are You Waiting for a Miracle?" *Kindred Spirit* (Fall 1979): 21-23.

Koop, C. Everett. "Faith Healing and the Sovereignty of God." *Tenth: An Evangelical Quarterly* (July 1976): 60-71.

Mavrodes, George I. "Bayes' Theorem and Hume's Treatment of Miracles." *Trinity Journal* 1 (1980): 47-61.

McCune, Rolland D. "A Biblical Study of Tongues and Miracles." *Central Bible Quarterly* 19 (Fall 1976): 6-22.

Mooneyham, W. Stanley. "Men Raised from the Dead? Water Turned into Wine?" *Moody Monthly* (November 1972): 90-95.

—. "What About the Miracles and Revival in Indonesia?" *Eternity* (November 1972): 18-20.

Mourant, John A. "Augustine on Miracles." *Augustinian Studies* 4 (1973): 103-27.

Mumper, Sharon E. "Where in the World Is the Church Growing?" *Christianity Today* (July 11, 1986): 17-21.

Phillips, John. "Miracles: Not for Today." *Moody Monthly* (July-August 1982): 72-74.

Power, David N. "Let the Sick Man Call." *The Heythrop Journal* 19 (July 1978): 256-70.

Richardson, Cyril C. "Spiritual Healing in the Light of History." *Pastoral Psychology* 5 (May 1954): 16-20.

Radmacher, Earl D., Ronald B. Allen, and H. Wayne House, eds. *Nelson's New Illustrated Bible Commentary* (Nashville: T. Nelson Publishers, 1999). 1 Cor 13:8-10.

Robbins, Dale A. "Healing is One of God's Benefits." *Victorious Publications.* Grass Valley, CA – Nashville. www.victorious.org/pub/receive-healing-116 (accessed November 29, 2018).

Ryrie, Charles C. "Greater Works Than These." *Good News Broadcaster* (June 1983): 32-34.

—. "Miracles (or What Happened to Your Handkerchiefs, Paul?)" *Moody Monthly* (September 1980): 82-85.

Scott, James W. "The Time When Revelatory Gifts Cease (1 Cor 13:8–12)." *Westminster Theological Journal* 72:2 (2010): 267-289.

Speigl, Jakob. "Early Christian Attitudes Toward Miracles." *Theology Digest* 19 (Autumn 1971): 254-257.

Stafford, Tim. "Testing the Wine from John Wimber's Vineyard." *Christianity Today* (August 8, 1986): 17-22.

Stone, Anthony P. "Christian Healing and Deliverance." *The TRACI Journal* 23 (September 1982): 4-13.

Taylor, G. Aiken. "Miracles—Yes or No?" *The Presbyterian Journal* 33 (August 14, 1974): 7-9.

Towns, Elmer L. "Does God Heal Today?" *The Fundamentalist Journal* 2 (June 1983): 36-38.

Unger, Merrill F. "Divine Healing." *Bibliotheca Sacra* 128 (July-September 1971): 234-44.

Van Dolson, Leo R. "When the Doctor is Baffled." *Ministry* 53 (May 1980): 20-21.

Wagner, C. Peter. "Healing Without Hassle." *Leadership* 6: 2 (Spring 1985): 114-15.

—. "Signs & Wonders: What difference do they make?" *Christian Life* (November 1982): 77-78.

—. "The Power of God and Your Power." *Christian Life* (July 1983): 40-46.

Whitcomb, John C., Jr. "Does God Want Christians to Perform Miracles Today?" *Grace Journal* 12 (Fall 1971): 2-12.

Wilcock, Michael. "The Apostle Paul and Healing." *Toward the Mark* (May-June 1983): 56-59.

Wilkinson, John. "Healing in the Epistle of James." *Scottish Journal of Theology* 24 (August 1971): 326-45.

Willmington, H. L. *Willmington's Bible Handbook*. Wheaton, IL: Tyndale House Publishers, 1997.

Witmer, John A. "The Doctrine of Miracles." *Bibliotheca Sacra* 130 (April-June 1973): 126-34.

Woods, Andy M. "The Meaning of the Perfect in 1 Corinthians 13:8–13." *Chafer Theological Seminary Journal* 10: 2 (2004): 3-31.

Unpublished Materials

Beals, Paul A. "The Significance of Miracles." ThM thesis, Dallas Theological Seminary, 1952.

Belch, Stephen L. "Paul's Life After the Close of Acts." ThM thesis, Dallas Theological Seminary, 1982.

Booth, John L. "The Purpose of Miracles." ThD dissertation, Dallas Theological Seminary, 1965.

Dane, Timothy L. "Maturity and Cessationism: The Cessation of the Revelatory Gifts with the Arrival of Body Maturity as Foretold by Paul in 1 Corinthians 13:8-13." PhD dissertation, Baptist Bible Seminary, 2016.

Dennis, Edward B. "The Duration of the 'charismata': An exegetical and theological study of 1 Corinthians 13:10." Master's thesis, Christian Broadcasting Network University, 1989.

Farnell, F. David. "The New Testament Prophetic Gift: Its Nature and Duration." PhD dissertation, Dallas Theological Seminary, 1990.

Forge, James N. "The Doctrine of Miracles in the Apostolic Church." ThM thesis, Dallas Theological Seminary, 1951.

Graber, John B. "The Temporary Gifts of the Holy Spirit." ThM thesis, Dallas Theological Seminary, 1947.

Hoehner, Harold. "Chronology of the Apostolic Age." ThD dissertation, Dallas Theological Seminary, 1965.

Martin, John A. "The Book of Acts" Unpublished class notes in 307 Acts and the General Epistles, Dallas Theological Seminary, Fall 1983.

Peterson, Brian G. "The Significance of Miracles within the Transitional Framework of the Book of Acts." ThM thesis, Dallas Theological Seminary, 1976.

Sterrett, T. Norton. "New Testament Charismata." ThD dissertation, Dallas Theological Seminary, 1947.

Sywulka, Paul E. "The Contribution of Hebrew 2:3-4 to the Problem of Apostolic Miracles." ThM thesis, Dallas Theological Seminary, 1967.

Witmer, John A. "The Biblical Doctrine of Healing." ThM thesis, Dallas Theological Seminary, 1946.

Appendix 1:
Problems of the Study

As with any study which bases its arguments on the relationship of biblical data to historical references and dating, there is the problem of placing both the miracles and the epistles within an acceptable chronological framework. This is compounded by the problem of dating the book of Hebrews whose reference to miracles as a past experience is critical in any argument for a decline or cessation of miracles within the New Testament era. To be useful, it must have been written after Paul's first Roman imprisonment. Lacking both a clear reference to author and date, the placement of the book is difficult to defend strongly. Even so, it must be placed relative to the other books.

A second difficulty lies in the chronology of the book of Acts and Paul's life with respect to miracles. Since Luke's record is not intended as a full biography or as a treatment of miracles, the presence of large time gaps between miracles within the record raises the question concerning actual gaps. Were there only certain times when Paul worked miracles? Did Luke only record significant ministries such as he had at Ephesus? Or, did Paul not always employ miracles as authenticating signs?

Finally, there is the use of silence in the argument for a decline or end to miracles. Does the silence of Paul's later epistles *actually* indicate a cessation, or just a lack of interest on the apostle's part? The silence of the record, by itself, would not be a compelling argument for the cessation of miracles, even when combined with the relative silence of the early church fathers. There must be more evidence than silence to develop a strong enough defense for such a position.

Appendix 2: Significance of the Study

The significance of the study is evident in light of the controversy concerning the permanence or transitional nature of miracles and certain spiritual gifts within God's program for the church. Within much of evangelicalism today is the belief that God should be working through miracles as much today as He did in the first century. One response which has been made is that miracles had an authenticating purpose which was fulfilled in the first century. They then declined and ceased with the completion of the canon and the death of the apostles' generation. Paul's three friends are provided as evidence of their cessation. If a decline can be demonstrated convincingly from Scripture, then solid ground exists to argue for their transitoriness. If it cannot be demonstrated, then this specific argument must be discarded and other answers formulated, such as their role in authentication.

As mentioned above, by demonstrating evidences of a decline in miracles and miracle-working ability, the position favoring their cessation is strengthened. This then provides an apologetic for arguing against a necessity for either modern miracle workers or a continuance of miracles in the numbers the first-century church experienced. Miller expresses the problem well when he says, "The real issue between the advocates of faith healing and those who oppose them is whether miraculous powers, such as were present in the apostolic period, were intended as essential and permanent structures in the church."[356] In providing evidence of a decline or cessation, the opponents of faith healing can more confidently state that those apostolic powers are no longer part of the church's experience, and those claiming them are either deceived or deceivers.

---

356 Waymon D. Miller, Modern Divine Healing, 302.

This study has sought to demonstrate that the decline is observable within the New Testament record and provides support for the belief that the presence of miracle workers performing miracles at will did indeed cease. It also strengthens the argument that the primary role of miracles, especially certain "sign gifts," was that of authentication and that their continuance was not expected even in the first century.

Appendix 3:
The Procedure of the Study

The scope of the study

This study was primarily limited to first century and biblical evidence, though some discussion of modern issues and evidence was incorporated into the argument. Still, this is primarily a historical/theological discussion. In that light, it was important to place the miracles of Acts and the epistles within a chronological framework, showing only a possible decline. The problem of Paul's three friends was addressed, placing them in relation to Paul's last recorded miracles. Then Paul's inability to heal them was discussed as it related to the question of a decline. The significance of the Hebrews 2 comment and the silence concerning miracles in the latter epistles is related to the non-faith healing position, along with the value of the argument of purpose in showing the silence to indicate a decline in light of Paul's friends' illnesses.

The limitations of the study

This study is limited in its consideration of miracles to the record of healing miracles involving an agent. Though such gifts as speaking in tongues should be considered miracles as well, healings obtained a greater interest in the record of Acts. Their use as examples of apostolic authentication, combined with the comments by Paul concerning men he could not heal, provide one aspect of the miraculous signs which is measurable throughout the rest of Scripture. This allows the study to do more than examine silences within the record. Since they served as one aspect of signs and wonders in the first century, and since the demonstrated decline of one aspect of miracle working would indicate at least the possibility of similar declines in others, their decline is being used as the measure for all miraculous gifts.

Because the apostolic period is under consideration, the Gospel records and post-apostolic writers will not be included in this study, though they are mentioned at one point. Keener's two-volume work provides ample extra-biblical data that can be evaluated by the reader. The nature of this book was such that only a minimal amount of space could be given to the post-New Testament era accounts. Also, though the Apostle John continued his ministry until near the end of the first century, his writings will not be used within the argument for a decline since they are so distantly removed from the other epistles chronologically. Their silence concerning miracles is noted, but not needed when measuring a decline. If a decline exists, it should be evident within Paul's lifetime.

ALSO AVAILABLE FROM LAMPION HOUSE PUBLISHING

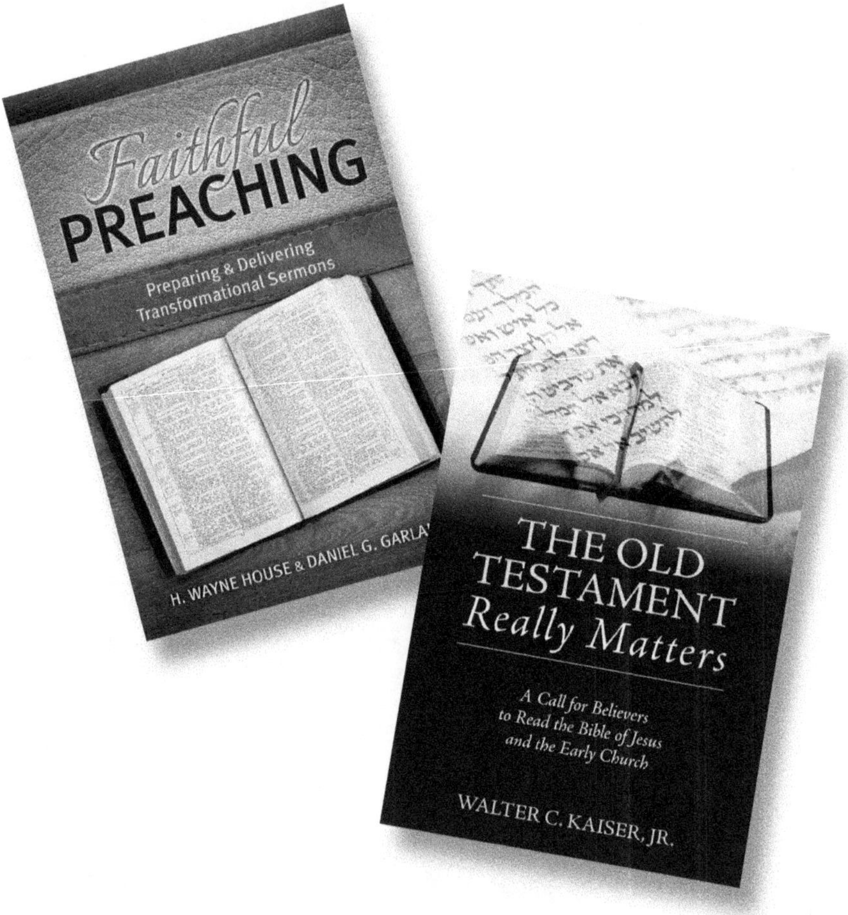

LOOK FOR THESE AND OTHER GREAT TITLES AT:

LAMPIONHOUSEPUBLISHING.COM

www.ingramcontent.com/pod-product-compliance
Lightning Source LLC
Chambersburg PA
CBHW070150100426
42743CB00013B/2868